PSYCHIC

Demystifying Our Hidden Human Potential

Fernando Marron

This work reflects actual events in the life of the author as truthfully as recollection permits. Some events have been compressed, and some dialogue has been recreated. While all persons within are actual individuals, names and identifying characteristics have been changed to protect their privacy.

Copyright 2025 by Fernando Marron

For more information, address:

info@fernandomarron.com

Paperback ISBN: 979-8-9928651-0-3

Ebook ISBN: 979-8-9928651-2-7

Hardcover ISBN: 979-8-9928651-1-0

www.FernandoMarron.com

FOREWORD

It is rare to encounter someone who not only embraces their psychic abilities but also commits to mastering them with such honesty and authenticity. Over the years, I have had the privilege of working with many gifted individuals, but Fernando stands out. His journey is not only deeply personal but also profoundly relatable.

When I first met Ferny, I immediately recognized his remarkable sensitivity and openness to learning, qualities that allowed him to sharpen and refine his natural abilities. What began as a flicker of curiosity quickly blossomed into a deeper commitment to understanding the intricacies of psychic phenomena. Watching him evolve from an eager student into a skilled practitioner, now guiding others on their own journeys has been an immensely rewarding experience as his proud mentor.

This book is a culmination of that journey—his and the collective quest of many who seek to understand their psychic potential. Fernando masterfully weaves together personal experiences, practical exercises, and insightful teachings to offer readers a roadmap for discovering and enhancing their own abilities. His approach is grounded, yet expansive; it is structured, yet allows for the intuitive flow that is so vital in this field.

What sets Fernando apart is not just his ability to connect with the psychic world but also his exceptional teaching. His methods are clear, accessible, and empowering, making it possible for beginners to feel confident in their psychic work.

Within these pages, you'll find exercises that challenge you to trust yourself, confront your fears, and embrace the unknown with courage. You will also find stories and insights that remind you that this path is one of both discovery and self-acceptance.

As a psychic and mentor, I have always believed that everyone possesses the ability to connect with their psychic senses. The challenge lies in cultivating belief and consistent practice. Fernando exemplifies the dedication required to unlock these abilities, and his work is a testament to the potential we all have to connect with the unseen.

As you read this book, approach it with an open heart and mind. Know that every step of this journey is one of learning, growth, and connection—both with the universe and with yourself. By the time you reach the final page, I am confident you will have gained a greater understanding of psychic phenomena but also a renewed trust in your inner guidance.

It has been my honor to mentor Fernando and to witness the evolution of his practice. I know this book will serve as a guiding light for anyone ready to embark on, or deepen their psychic journey.

Pam Coronado
Psychic Detective, Intuitive Reader, Spiritual Teacher

TABLE OF CONTENTS

CHAPTER 1

Awakening Psychic Ability

Growing up, people always called me sensitive. It's true. I was a sensitive child. Trauma can do that. To survive, I had to be keenly attuned to others' needs. I always needed to be aware of potential danger and how to diffuse it, constantly sensing and processing the world around me. Hypervigilance helped me survive as a young, gay boy from a Catholic family in the East Side of Houston in the 1980s. My walls were up so high that even I couldn't see over them. I spent a lot of my early childhood alone, safe behind the walls of the one-bedroom apartment I shared with my single mother, confiding more in imaginary friends than in real people. Well, sharing more of my experiences with what I'd been conditioned to believe were "imaginary friends" than with real people.

Today, I am a sensitive adult. I'm proud of that fact. Sensitivity is the greatest tool a person can possess, especially for anyone with psychic abilities. My sensitivity–my ability to be keenly attuned to the world outside of myself–allowed me to be open to supernatural experiences that profoundly affected the rest of my life. Those experiences completely altered my understanding of human potential. They are the reason that I am a professional Psychic Medium today.

Beyond me, though, harnessing sensitivity is the first step in the path for *anyone* seeking to access their full human potential, including their psychic potential. That's right. You can be psychic. You can awaken your psychic abilities. You can open your mind to the awesomeness of the infinite universe and its infinite possibilities. You can break free from the shackles of societal norms to welcome an entirely different realm of experience. To be psychic, you have to be willing to be sensitive and to work on your skills. *Anyone* can be psychic.

A Perfect Storm

Let's rewind. My mother and father met in a hotel room for a secret tryst. My father was a married man going through a divorce when he came across my mother, a young, devout, Catholic woman. As they did some old-fashioned Catholic sinning, engaging in premarital sex, the mirror in the bathroom shattered and broke as they reached climax. My dad disappeared, and my mother went on believing that the shattered mirror was a message from her deceased mother that she was being a naughty girl. They never stopped to challenge those notions rooted in Puritanism and fear to explore the other possibilities of what that earth-shaking energy could have been.

That energy was me. My mom would go on to raise me alone. She thought about getting an abortion, but, in a dream, her mother commanded her, "This child must be born." So, shortly thereafter, I entered the world. One morning, my mother heard me laughing alone in my crib. Curious, she followed the noise, my faint laughter drawing her closer. Amid the darkness stood a figure, bathed in white light, enrobed in a long, pink dress gazing downward into the crib. The figure spoke to my mother. "I will send you an angel to take care of him." My mother gazed upon the face of the woman bathed in light. It was her mother–the same one she feared felt disappointed in her–giving her a great blessing. In turn, my grandmother blessed me, too. My mom, no matter the circumstances she'd be under, would always find a way to make things work out for us.

The unusual circumstances of my birth shaped my evolution into a peculiar child. Often, my older cousin, Monica, would babysit me while my mom worked long into the night. Monica hardly needed to do anything while babysitting because I'd easily occupy myself. I would spend hours sitting on the floor, staring attentively at a grand, vintage, thoroughly worn Victorian-style chair made of deep brown wood and faded sienna cushioning. At times, I'd nod my head, as if someone in the chair were imparting wisdom directly to me, and I was an eager sponge, ready to absorb every bit. Other times, I'd be fully engaged with an imaginary friend, gesticulating wildly to the static air in front of the wall.

In elementary school, I would eschew the gender-based dynamics that rule children of a certain age. Instead of participating in the "boy" activities, I'd attempt to assign roles to the girls in my kindergarten class–ordering one to start slicing bread, the other to set the table, one to fold the napkins, and one to fill the cups–so we could make "lunch" for the boys. I was so noticeably different from the molds available for Texas children that, out of necessity, I was emboldened to be myself.

But, as the curiosity of a child is slowly siphoned away by the pedantic mores of a parent, I too learned to fear, to hide, and to keep secrets. I was made to learn to suppress my feelings, my thoughts, and my eccentricities. I was made to feel like an outcast–like I didn't fit with the world around me–and to feel shame for that. I was made to think that the world around me operated in this preordained, highly regimented way. There was the word of the Church and the word of my friends, family, and peers. Neither dictionary had the vocabulary to define who I was, so the world tried to make me fit into other words.

When I was about six, I was at the bus stop, playing with a Mickey Mouse toy from a cereal box, as my mom and I waited for the bus outside of the Dollar Store. The bus doors opened, but instead of getting on board, a strange man with a suitcase came down the stairs and walked over to us. My mom greeted him, looked at me and said, "This is your new dad. He lives with us now." The one-bedroom apartment added a new occupant, my stepfather, followed closely by a new sister and, about three years later, another sister. My stepfather took a while to settle into our home but, once he did, his true nature emerged. He was soft with my sisters–gentle and nurturing. But to my mom and me, he was a monster. He'd drink late into the night, fueling his anger and aggression. He'd beat me for not being his son. He'd beat me for being too effeminate–that was something I shouldn't have dared to be in our very religious, Hispanic community. He'd beat my mom in front of me. He'd call us nasty words, degrade us, and yell until our humanity sloughed from our spirits.

I existed in a constant state of fear and loneliness. My stepfather *was* toxic masculinity, and he took every chance he could to show me I was not enough. I didn't feel safe anywhere. My mom was supposed to be my protector, but she was valuing a relationship with my tormentor over my wellbeing. School, which at one time I looked to as a respite, became another layer of torment. The boys could tell I was different and teased me, calling me "faggot" or "queer." I didn't know what those words meant, but I knew they hurt. Sometimes the girls accepted me, and I'd eagerly join them any time I was invited to lunch. Other times, I'd be an interference with their girls-only space. I felt utterly alone.

In my loneliness, I'd occasionally dream that my dad would come back and take me away. I imagined he would understand my distress, ease it with a hug, and carry me into a new life. On my seventh birthday, my mom and aunts threw me a Teenage Mutant Ninja Turtles themed birthday party. We didn't have the money for the official merchandise, but my aunts' creativity and skill produced handmade turtle t-shirts for everyone in attendance. Mine, of course, was Donatello–he was the smart one, after all. The one that didn't use lethal self-defense. He was a dreamer, just like me.

During this party, my dream was going to come true. I was going to meet my father. He was going to come at noon. When noon passed, he was on his way, going to get there in the afternoon. When the afternoon passed, his car supposedly got a flat, but he was still going to make it before the party ended. As the party ended, I waited on the garage apartment steps outside my grandpa's house, watching the setting sun drench the sky with a beautiful ribbon of pink and orange.

Numb, heartbroken, and disappointed, I sat on my grandpa's stoop. A sharp pang ricocheted through my heart as every star that appeared in the night sky confirmed what I already knew: he wasn't coming, and he would never come. As we arrived home later in the evening, my skin grew hot with waves of anger lapping at my consciousness.

I'd cried about my father before, especially when running home from school after being mercilessly teased by the kids my age—maybe this is why he did not want to be part of my life. But that night, not a tear would fall. In fact, never again would I cry over my father. When I woke up in the morning, I decided to never live life from a place of grief. If this man didn't want to meet me, or come to see the incredible shirts my aunts made, then that was firmly his loss. Sorry not sorry, Dad.

Eventually, my mom left the monster with the suitcase. A few months after my baby sister was born and after another failed attempt at AA for my stepfather, my mom decided to leave him. She called my grandfather. He drove up with his big truck, loaded my mother, my sisters, and me inside, and we rode away for good.

But leaving him broke her, leaving her more vulnerable than ever and needing my help more than ever. The divorce proceedings were my stepfather's final serving of torture. During the proceedings, he'd follow her, telling her how he'd hurt her–kill her–if she ever left. That thought haunted her. She spiraled into a mental breakdown, as her mind clouded with hallucinations and voices. Instead of trying to figure out what was wrong with her, my family decided she was possessed by the devil and took her to a priest for an exorcism. After a failed exorcism, my aunt, practicing witchcraft, attempted a fix. That, too, failed. Herbal supplements failed. Teas failed.

Eventually, with all other options exhausted, my family finally took her to a hospital, and she was diagnosed with schizophrenia. Next came the drugs. My mom, once the loudest person in the room, became a scooped–out version of herself. She bounced between various homes and mental institutions for a while. She used to have this hearty, warm laugh that filled the ears and oozed joy. It was the type of laugh that made other people laugh. A laugh that turns strangers into friends. I have yet to hear that laugh in my adult life.

My sisters were shipped off to live with other family members, leaving me to care for my mother. I stepped up to be the man of the family. The drugs frequently zombified my mother. Still, we found ourselves in a period of relative stability. A fortuitous entry into the 12 Days of Christmas contest led to us winning a house full of furniture. We ended up moving onto my uncle's property, and we made a home. I finally had a safe space where I could feel, where I could be alone, and where no one was going to bother me for being myself. My heavily medicated mother frequently alternated between sleeping and sitting for hours while staring lifelessly at the TV.

When she'd go through transition periods between new meds, she'd quickly relapse and revert back to unhealthy thoughts. Her sisters would talk amongst themselves about how she just wanted attention. But she'd confide in me scary thoughts, like the urge to grab a knife to plunge into those closest to her and herself, ripping through the bodies of her loved ones, and about her physical pain when she'd get muscle spasms from the medication withdrawals. She'd cry out to me, and I'd run over, desperately trying to straighten her neck to keep her muscles from locking into an uncomfortable position or just sitting with her as she stared at the popsicle stick house she made during therapy. Even though I lacked an understanding of what schizophrenia really meant, I believed my mom. I felt her pain, and I did my best to give her the safety and comfort she needed.

The First Opening

The best part about being in a place of stability was that I had the luxury of being bored. Since I didn't have many friends, I'd be alone a lot, sitting around and thinking. As a boy ushering in his teenage years, a lot of that thinking had to do with hormones. I'd also deeply contemplate the vastness of the universe, the essence of God, the meaning of life–I'd think about everything and nothing. I explored the depths of my mind.

When the silence was too deafening, I'd turn on the TV to have some familiar chatter as background noise. One evening, the cadence of the chatter departed from its regular schedule. My ears perked up, picking up bits and pieces of what was unfolding on the TV. Captivated and curious, I began to watch.

I grew up Catholic, but the ideologies taught by my faith and belief system left me with more questions than answers. The priests grew tired of my constant inquiries, often resorting to quick deflections or vague responses in an attempt to distract me from their uncertainty. As a teenager beginning to understand my attraction to men, I drifted even further away from the Church. The Church constantly told me that my sexuality would make me evil or a threat to the world, and the Church spread that poisonous idea to its followers.

Once, I was spending time with my favorite cousin, and I told her that a book I'd read said that sometimes people are born gay because they were meant to experience life with a unique perspective. This idea helped me feel like I had a place in the world that I could not find within the Church.

No sooner than I expressed vulnerability with her did she turn ice cold. Her lifelong conditioning, pouring over religious texts, finding a community in Church, obeying the commandments, and trusting the priest over her own judgment, rose from her. She could not comprehend how I could possibly believe that I was the male reincarnation of a soul that lived lifetimes as a woman. My beliefs were outside of the closed circle of her world. "That's not true. You just want to believe that because you don't want to believe what the Bible says is going to happen to you." She wasn't saying it with hate or the conviction that I was repulsive and going to hell; she just couldn't imagine anyone believing in any alternative to the Church's teachings. In her mind, I was choosing to ignore reality. Years later, she apologized for not being more accepting of me, but the feeling of being condemned by my family and faith was still the same. I may not have opened my cousin to new beliefs back then, but I'd positioned myself in a new reality.

The Church was not my place. The rules were too rigid, the perspective too narrow. I knew there was more, and I knew I didn't need a Church to have a relationship with God. Priests couldn't give me the answers I sought about God, so why was I listening to them? Clearly, I did not have the best track record of adhering to the status quo, so why was I still trying to please it?

When the new chatter of the TV called, I listened. I discovered a new, albeit fictional world on a show called Star Trek Voyager. It was unlike anything I'd ever seen before. New worlds, new languages, new technobabble! But what really caught my attention was this character, Kes, a young girl from a race of people called the "Ocampa." The Ocampa were rumored to have extraordinary psychic powers, and the show follows Kes as she begins to become aware of her own power. The more I'd watch her explore her powers, the more my ideas on the limits of human potential were challenged.

Instead of focusing on "why," I began focusing on "what if." "Why" explains the present by looking at the past. "What if" explores the future by understanding the present. All that trauma I'd survived helped me to understand the human condition in a deeply significant way. It taught me how to sense danger. The rejection and isolation taught me to embrace the fullness of my difference. My sexuality challenged the essential tenets of my religion. I knew "why" I was, but "what if" I could be more?

Star Trek caused a rapid expansion of my thoughts. With a rapid expansion came new connections, new openings for ideas, and new experiences. My conception of the world began to change. As it shifted, I entered into a new era of interacting with the supernatural that would lay the groundwork for my life.

A Fire Inside

It was a Saturday. I was about 13 years old, my favorite movie was Jurassic Park, and I had no idea what a psychic was. My mom and I had been in a stable position for quite some time. We were experiencing life above suffering. She was in a mental place where, despite still being a zombie, she maintained a job at the local pita factory part-time, leaving me alone often. I was proud of her for being able to get up, go to work every day, and keep that job. A bonus was that I could watch as many Saturday morning cartoons as I desired while she was away at work, of which I definitely took advantage. I'd make myself breakfast, play with toys, or lie on my bed with my feet on the wall and eyes toward the ceiling. Saturday mornings were my time to be fully free–no school, no obligations. Just me and the endless possibilities of my mind.

Walking toward the fridge on the way to start making myself a snack, I began to experience a vivid memory of an event that never happened. It was deja vu before I understood what deja vu really was. The vision was so clear, as though I was standing in my kitchen and the stove was against the wall to my left, just like it always was. Flanked on one side were these large, wooden cabinets in a deep, rich brown. I stared at the room from the entryway, watching it fill with thick, black smoke. Flames spouted from the stove, stretching onto the deep brown cabinets, dancing in front of my eyes. Smoke billowed from the room. Our house was in danger–I was in danger.

PSYCHIC

I stood paralyzed, mid-stride, trying to understand what I was experiencing. While I was in the kitchen at that moment, this fire that appeared so vividly in my mind was not happening and had never happened. A voice that sounded like my own, only much calmer and wiser, came forth inside of my head. The voice asked me, "What would you do if this happened? If there was a fire blazing in front of you?" As the voice faded, I considered the answer for a few moments. I don't know why, but I knew that I had to create a plan of action to counteract such an event. We'd never had a fire, but "what if?" What if I had a chance to save our house from burning down?

The wheels turned in my head. What if I came into the kitchen and there were a fire spouting from the stove, leaping from cabinet to cabinet, crawling across the wall, threatening the home where we finally felt peace and stability? I would walk into the kitchen. With the stove to my left, I'd charge over to the sink affixed to the wall directly across from the entrance, holding my breath the entire time. Grabbing the faucet sprayer, I'd pull it as far as it goes to hose down the fire before it started spreading from cabinet to cabinet. Then, after extinguishing the fire, I'd turn and run to the leftmost corner of the room, opening the door to let both me and the smoke vacate the room. Finally, once outside and safe from the blaze, I'd inhale again. This would give me the best chance to save myself and our home.

I practiced the routine at least a couple of times each day for the next two weeks, running through the steps each time I'd step into the kitchen to make a snack. This "memory" now seared into my mind would not become a reality on my watch.

And so, it was Saturday morning two weeks later. My mom left for work, and I went into the kitchen to whip up some pancakes. After finishing cooking, I turned off the stove and moved the pan over to the cool coils I hadn't used. Our stove faithfully prepared the food, as usual; however, as an old hand-me-down, turning the knob to the off position did not guarantee that the stove itself would power down after preparing a meal. The alignment had to be just right for the stove to recognize the command to stop. When I'd finished cooking, the stubborn stove still gave off significant heat, causing me to adjust the knob until it was clear that the stove was no longer on. Our smoke alarm blared, but this was the usual course when we cooked–we didn't have a stove vent, and someone thought it was wise to put the smoke detector directly above the stove on the wall, sounding with the slightest wisp of smoke or steam from even the most routine cooking.

The aroma of the pancakes filled my nose as I shuffled with the plate back to my room. Alarm still wailing, I began digging into my food, unfazed and engrossed by the cartoons on the screen. That same voice I'd recognized as my own called out to me quietly and clearly, "Fernando, go to the kitchen." I was a teenager, though, and I had a predilection for dismissing the advice of a parent. Through the ringing, I persisted in watching my show. The voice grew louder and its tone changed: "Fernando, go to the kitchen." I responded to the voice inside my head, fully in conversation inside myself. "No, I don't want to go to the kitchen. I want to watch my show and eat my breakfast." A third time, the voice bellowed: "FERNANDO! GO TO THE KITCHEN!" No longer was this just a suggestion; it was a command. Begrudgingly, I trudged over to the kitchen.

What I saw shook me to my core. It was the exact scenario that appeared to me two weeks before. Smoke billowed from the stove, cascading out into the entryway. Flashes of light jumped from the fire, extending from our hand-me-down stove. Despite preparing for this exact scenario for days, I still panicked. No sooner than I regained enough composure to ask myself what to do was I racing to the sink, holding my breath almost reflexively, and carrying out the plan exactly as I'd practiced it. I extinguished the fire before running outside to catch my breath. Taking a gulp of the outside air, I tried to understand what happened–did I really just go through that?!

We didn't call the police or the fire department–that was not the programmed response for a poor family in the hood of Houston. Instead, I called out to my Tio that lived next door. He dropped the phone, running over to the scene of the fire. He was immediately relieved, happy that the house didn't burn down and that I was okay. We removed the stove shortly thereafter. It had lost our trust, and that memory was not going to have the opportunity to repeat itself.

My ability to sense the kitchen fire was an example of the extent of my human potential. When reflecting on the incident, I realized the voice that popped into my head, while sounding like me, was not my own. Instead, it was closer to a supernatural occurrence–it was a connection to something higher than my being, more knowledgeable than I, imparting information that was otherwise unexplainable.

The following week, another experience reinforced my burgeoning understanding of what was happening to me, first discovered in the wake of the fire. It was Thursday, and my mom was in the kitchen preparing dinner for me, my Aunt Melba, and my cousin Jennifer. They were already in the kitchen serving themselves when my mom called me over to eat. As I made my way through the doorway, I suddenly stopped in my tracks and announced, "The lights are going to go off." The words came to me, free from a discernable origin and untethered to any concrete experience. It wasn't raining–no thunder clapped, and there was no lightning in the sky. Still confused by the words that rolled out of my mouth, my mom began scolding me: "You shouldn't say things like that. It's bad luck." My aunt said saying things like that would call the evil eye.

But, just a few moments later, the power for the entire block went off. I turned to my mom and aunt to witness them reconciling both a sense of fear and awe. My cousin giggled, saying the whole thing was funny. She asked, "How did you know that was going to happen?" I told her that I had no idea. We later found out that the transformer for the neighborhood blew, causing a power outage; but, in that moment, I knew that something was shifting inside of me.

Just like Kes, I was undergoing an evolution in my nature. While I did not understand it, I wanted to explore it. My journey had begun. What I share in these next chapters is what I've come to understand from passionate study, years of self-exploration, and the direct experience in developing the use of my psychic ability.

CHAPTER 2

WHAT YOU NEED TO KNOW

Before we delve any further into what it means to be psychic, let's stop.

The following is what I wish I had known before beginning my psychic journey. Remember these as you read this book. Allow your expectations to melt away as they will not serve you moving forward.

There's an elephant in the room that we need to address. And it sees dead people. Or maybe it doesn't...

Most people have no idea what it means to be psychic or have psychic ability because their comprehension is rooted firmly in depictions of psychics in media, especially fiction.

What is Psychic Ability?

Psychic ability does not mean you speak in riddles or parables. It does not mean you are a godlike or omnipotent being. Psychics don't have the power to instantly change people's lives. Psychics are not wise sages with the knowledge of every era of time. A psychic is not a magician. A psychic is a person.

Psychic ability is the capability of a person to engage all of their sensory facilities to understand the world as it appears to them.

Notice: I said, "of a person," not "of a psychic." Why is that?

Because everyone is psychic! **You are psychic!** Congratulations! That tingle that runs down your spine when you know something bad is going to happen...and it does...That urge you get to call a friend for the first time in three years, and when they answer, the first words they say are, "I was just about to call you!" Those are psychic events.

Intuition is the most common psychic event–the ability to intuit exists latent in everyone. We all possess intuition as a skill.

Intuition for a given person may be sharper in a specific area. Imagine a stockbroker. He spends his life staring at screens, reviewing investment prospectuses, and assessing value. Whether actively or not, he is constantly processing information through his expertise. His *intuition* on where to invest will be clearer than mine because his psychic ability is more acute: all that he's already seen allows him to see more. As a result, the more he can use his intuition to form his predictions, the more accurate his predictions will become.

But, one need not be a stockbroker to make accurate predictions in the world of stocks. Intuition is a byproduct of fixation. The stockbroker's fixation cues him into more attributes when making his predictions. Anyone, though, can educate themselves to help strengthen their intuitive abilities in the area. The stockbroker may have an advantage in making accurate predictions because of their background, but anyone can learn.

No one person is more worthy, special, or deserving of psychic capabilities. The difference between practicing psychics and everyone else is…practice. The willingness to hone the skill is the difference between the layman and the practicing psychic.

That does not mean that now, after discovering that you have psi (or psychic) ability, you should go out into the world armed with a tarot deck and start charging for readings. There is a responsibility inherent in psi ability and in calling yourself a psychic because the words of a psychic, although not a divine word, are stronger than mere advice or comfort. The duty of those who wish to use their psi ability to affect others is to engage in training and to use their skills responsibly.

Psychics are Not Magic

A psychic cannot levy a curse, and a psychic cannot cure a curse. This is a misconception promoted by Charlatans looking to exploit others for monetary gain by giving a magical explanation that removes personal responsibility and will all but guarantee future visits.

I will say this once: no sentient being on this planet has the right or ability to control the life of another using any form of "magic."

I frequently get calls, emails, and messages from folks who believe they are cursed, asking me if I can remove the curse and change the trajectory of their lives. No, you are not cursed. And no, I do not have a magic wand that can change your life. Most importantly, I will not take your money to tell you that you do, and that I can.

It's far easier for a person to believe in a curse than to believe that they have made bad choices. A curse removes agency. It acts on you without your consent. It robs you of your agency and punishes you without reason. That feels pretty powerful, right…

But the reality is that sometimes, your significant other left not because of a curse, but because they wanted to. No one was magically pulling their energetic strings, like a puppeteer in Pinocchio, and forced them to leave. Maybe they didn't like you after they got to know you or maybe they preferred the company of someone else. Regardless, they didn't want to be with you, so they chose to leave. It was not the power of an ancient curse that has been following your family for centuries.

For many I know, it is much easier to go to a self-proclaimed Shaman or Curandero (for my Hispanic folks) than to do the hard work of looking inward, admitting mistakes, seeking therapy, and changing behaviors. A Shaman will charge you a few hundred or thousand dollars to perform some rituals or sell you some junk to make you feel like a change happened *around* you; a therapist will charge you a few hundred or thousand dollars to make *you* change.

Only one of those outcomes is sustainable; the other one is a con.

And in our world, as long as the psychic industry is unregulated, we will have these con artists. Some really do believe they have magical powers, but regardless, they all run around fooling people into giving up their money without much evidence or merit.

While people *may* leave themselves open to certain energy patterns and waves, which is the closest thing to a "curse" I've encountered, these are not actually curses. Don't worry, we'll get to discussing those, too.

Psychics Can Be Catty

Again, if we are all psychic, then psychics are not, by definition, special. Unfortunately, psychics are all still very much human and are besieged by the pesky nuisance called ego.

Certainly, many psychics act like rabid dogs fighting to the death over limited resources. Every psychic with a different skill set than their own is a threat that needs to be diminished, discounted, or discredited. Psychics are constantly trying to break each other down, fueled by spite, pettiness, and competitiveness. Psychics are pettier than middle school girls with mean streaks made of ego instead of changing hormones. That means psychics tend to stay petty.

With the advent of personality-driven psychic TV series, many psychics feel like they're dueling constantly to be America's (or the International) Next Great Psychic. When you have people running around trying to be the next Theresa Caputo, John Edward, or Sylvia Browne, you'll certainly meet people who will try to make you look and sound like an amateur to try to improve their profile in comparison. Instead of working harder on themselves, they seem to work harder on throwing people under the bus. It's happened to me more than once.

But it's not just the lack of professional courtesy. Like any filter, ego can have effects on the ability to perform the task of a psychic accurately and adequately. When clouded by the goal of being "big," predictions can take the form of satisfying the psychic's aims more than giving the client a quality reading.

Psychics need to remember that they are not participating in the Hunger Games; there's enough skill to go around, enough space to develop further, and enough opportunities to affect real change in people's lives (even without a syndicated television show).

Psychics Don't Know Everything

A psychic does not "know." A psychic predicts.

I am a psychic. I am *not* a fortune teller. I am a person that senses details about the past, present, and future. I can interpret the information received to provide a prediction of how that information will be represented in a person's life. I am not a crystal ball.

The all-knowing psychic is a great image, but, in reality, it's a myth perpetuated by the media, opportunists capitalizing on vulnerable people, and ignorant people who have not studied the actual phenomenon in any significant detail. Psychics can only understand and gain awareness of things through their ordinary and "extraordinary" sensory capabilities. If psychics knew the future with absolute certainty and 100% accuracy, a lot more of them would be lottery winners. We'll discuss this more in Chapter 9 on Prophetic Dreams.

A Mind's Eye? Psychic Sensing and Visual Memory

It is difficult for many psychics to explain how they work, what they're experiencing, and how it can relate to scientific examples. In an effort to relate their mental processes to others, they frequently resort to using very literal language to make the abstract more concrete. The result is misleading language like "seeing through the mind's eye," a phrase which is taken to mean seeing a movie play out before them in their minds. That then becomes the experience most closely related to being psychic. If there's no movie playing in your head, then you aren't psychic! Then, the average person–and remember, none of us are special without working on our skills–cannot even conceive that they should attempt to work on their skills because the inside of their eyelids don't double as projector screens. This language discourages people from attempting to discover their skills, redefining psi ability as exclusive instead of inclusive.

Don't close your eyes. Think of what you ate today for breakfast. Delicious. Hold onto that memory and let it luxuriate. You can see it, can't you? You can see the image of the food you ate for breakfast. You can see the eggs cooked over-easy, sitting on a slice of sourdough bread. Or maybe you just had a coffee or a protein shake. That memory you conjured is visual memory. Put simply, that is clairvoyance. That is psychic sensing. The only thing that makes that sandwich in your head different from real psychic sensing is that you are triggering the memory yourself. When you begin to practice real psychic sensing, the visual memory will be triggered as the mind attempts to relay pertinent information. There is no movie playing–no Bruce Willis realizing he's a ghost–there is just the very simple process of clairvoyance using visual memory. With time and practice, the mind will shift away from visual memory and more toward visual psychic sensing that provides a more detailed and accurate depiction of the situation or target of your thoughts.

The manifestation of psi ability is not a monolith. Not every psychic exercises their skills in the same way. In fact, many psychics possess completely different sets of skills.

The Hollywood Psychic

The Sixth Sense nestled into public consciousness in 1999. The audience saw the world through the eyes of Cole Sear, this soft-spoken, young, and troubled boy played by Haley Joel Osment (Get it? See-er?). His bright eyes would near tears as he grappled with graphic images of dead people hanging from the rafters of his school and played in a tent with a pre-OC Mischa Barton, deceased after being poisoned by her mother. This child's amazing talents piqued the public's curiosity, especially as it was revealed in the coda of the film that his therapist, a child psychologist played by Bruce Willis, was actually a ghost refusing to cross over during the entire course of the film.

As soon as "I see dead people" entered the lexicon, every third psychic would publicly pronounce that they were the real-life Cole Sear. They could communicate with the dead and help them cross over. They would promote themselves by stating how closely their talents aligned with what the little boy could do in the film. This bad habit even infected true industry professionals. They wanted to capitalize on the public fascination to gain capital for themselves. These prolific claims caused the perception of what a "psychic" was to shift into a monolith—a psychic did what Cole Sear did in *The Sixth Sense*, of course. Hollywood said it, so this must be what it looks like in real life, the logic followed. Hollywood's standard became the industry standard.

This was not the last misleading portrayal of psychic ability in popular media. Unfortunately, "shock value" sells tickets. Producers care about getting people to leave their homes for the spectacle of the theater, not about telling a true and nuanced story about the work of a psychic. Accuracy is boring. A boy who can see dead bodies is not! Most psychic processes are mental, occurring almost entirely within the psychic's mind. That makes for a much less interesting visual story than a pale girl violently throwing up in a tent before disappearing.

What is a Psychic? What is a Medium? What is a Cole Sear?

Both psychics and mediums function in the same way: they engage in sensing things. Whereas all mediums are psychic, not all psychics are mediums. Being a medium requires special attention to communication—a fixation with the energy *around* a person instead of within the person. In focusing on the energy *around* a person, it is possible to connect with the thoughts and energy of a person that used to be in a different physical body.

When a client asks to connect with a specific individual, it's as if the client has picked up the phone. But it's not words being communicated—it's the spirit's intention, and the messaging comes through the triggering of thoughts, memories, emotions, and bodily sensations. Let's call it "phone charades." Communicating with the energy around the client allows the medium, as the phone receiver, to access the client's phone book, permitting the medium to place a call through the energy frequency emitted by the client thinking about their loved one. Then, the medium connects and interprets the message for the client.

Even in death, we are all connected.

So, is Cole Sear in *The Sixth Sense* a medium? Yes. An energy presence need not be intentionally summoned; it may be felt without any input. A medium is always a conduit for energy reception. Building on the analogy of the phone, a spirit-initiating connection with a medium is an incoming call. A medium's energy phone can ring without a client in three primary ways: (1) like a telemarketer soliciting any open line, a spirit wishing to connect seeking anyone available to talk; (2), like a wrong number dial, a spirit reaching initiating communication but failing to find its intended recipient; or (3), like a butt dial, a spirit initiating communication without realizing what they're doing—an unconscious reaching out.

At the same time, when the intention to connect emits from a client, the medium, too, may receive unsolicited calls—but these are typically from people already in their clients' phonebooks. Suddenly, the medium is connected with someone the client did not seek; however, the spirit craved communication so deeply or so desperately needed to impart a message that they intercepted the client's energy signal.

Cole Sear would be an "open line that constantly receives telemarketers and wrong numbers." At least at the beginning of *The Sixth Sense*, he didn't have a large enough rolodex for butt-dials.

Different Strokes for Different Folks: The Flavors of Psychics

Not every psychic is the same. Not every psychic will have the same predictions. Not every psychic practices the same way. Not every psychic has the same set of skills or experience. And not every psychic can give you what you want or need.

People are *obsessed* with the idea that all psychics operate the same and have the same skill set. They see the depictions of psychics on television and default to thinking, "Okay, they all work like that," instead of noticing the patterns in what types of psychics are showcased. Granted, if you go to enough developed and competent psychics, you'll encounter a continuity in their predictions or perceptions regarding events and circumstances. But often I've had clients disagree with me on my predictions or details I've sensed because other psychics told them something else. I inform the client that I am not the same as those psychics, nor do I sense things the same way they do, and I honor what I get. I'm not in the habit of validating someone else's predictions or perceptions, and how I do what I do *is* how *I DO WHAT I DO*. My job as a psychic is not to tell a client what they want to hear—it's to see what's in front of me, regardless of whether it will feel good for me to say it or for them to hear it. I provide a service, and I will provide it compassionately *especially* if it is something that may be hard to hear, but I do not perform magic.

Each psychic will sense things differently because each psychic is as unique as the human being they are. Each psychic will have differing abilities about the level of detail they can perceive, largely dependent on their skill set and the amount of time they spend developing their ability. A more trained psychic will likely be able to distinguish finer details when they "tune in."

Furthermore, the psychic's ability to "tune in" to certain details is greatly informed by the psychic's actual experiences. A psychic who used to be a doctor will likely be more adept at picking up on specific medical occurrences or conditions during a read. A former accountant may be able to reach greater specifics around numbers within their readings. There's a medium in England who spent decades as a mailman; he can tell you first and last names, addresses, and so on when connecting to the deceased.

Because I grew up as a Star Trek and tech nerd, educating myself constantly on the latest trends, I am especially adept at sensing technology-related specifics during my readings. My mind is more primed to grasp and comprehend things related to those spheres where I have a lot of knowledge. Another psychic might love reality TV and drama, which allows them to precisely outline what's happening in a relationship during a reading, demonstrating an understanding of how it will trend and progress. For me, though, I couldn't care less about whether Sarah pissed off her mother-in-law so much that she will be cut out of the will, so that detail may be less likely to pop up in my psyche when making a prediction.

Psychics have specialties, just like other professions. If an individual knows what they are seeking in a psychic, they may find their optimal match in terms of skills and specialties ensuring they receive the best reading possible. It's unlikely for me to be the best psychic to tell Sarah the street address of her mother-in-law's will so she can find it and destroy it. But another psychic could be a fit for that task.

Psychic Ability Is Rooted in Psychic Belief

Just like psychics have different specialties, psychics have different perspectives. Psychics come from all over the world, are steeped in every different culture, are raised in every type of situation, and are grown in all walks of life. Because of this, many skilled psychics can say the same things in different ways.

We all have filters that shape how we see the world.

Imagine a shiny, red apple.

What's the first connection you make? Your first thought?

For a scientist, it could be deciding what type of apple it is–let's get the species so we can begin to have an informed discussion. That's a delicious apple, hopefully.

For the deeply religious, it may conjure up images of Adam and Eve, representing original sin and expulsion from the Garden of Eden. That's a powerful apple.

For a woman who loved to cook with her grandmother, that's an apple that will end up in Sunday night's pie, a treat for when her extended family gets together once a week. That's a sentimental apple.

For a hungry person, it may conjure up more hunger or lead to feelings of resentment.

For me, well, my first thought is Snow White and the Evil Queen. Her name was actually Evil Queen, and that apple is poison.

For another, the apple may not be able to be conjured because there is no reference point. That apple is an oddly shaped red ball.

All that to say, we all have different meanings for different things and our cultures and backgrounds have contributed to this. When most people begin to develop their psychic abilities, they'll develop them through the lens of their background and cultural references. These lenses become the filters through which readings are done– they become the apple-colored glasses of psychic ability. While initial sensing exercises will be heavily impacted by established filters, over time, filters will diminish, and the sensory perceptions will gain more vivid details.

Remember these filters, especially when beginning practice, because it may help stop any impulse to compare your practice to everyone else. Both you and your filters are valid.

Still, why is psychic ability not taken seriously?

Given the conditioning we receive from a young age, it is easier to exist in a world where everything is plainly understood and in alignment with an individual's beliefs, experiences, and desires. It is easier to exist in a reality with the illusion of control—where things that fall outside of one's beliefs may simply be disparaged as being frivolous instead of interrogated for their potential value.

People who are adaptive, amenable, and open to emotional sensitivity are better suited to have psychic experiences. With culture demanding that women be more amenable, malleable, and observant, they develop the skills to adapt quickly to shifting emotionally and mentally impactful experiences.

In a patriarchal society built around the needs of men, shaped by the thoughts of men, and formulated to maintain the power of men, it's unsurprising that something like psychic ability, which challenges the conventional way of thinking, seems more likely to reject psychic ability. Psychic ability derives power from something other than the patriarchy, existing beyond its control, so the patriarchy will seek to delegitimize it to neutralize its power.

In general, men tend to reject the usefulness of activities dominated by women or that champion "feminine" values. Thus, with psychic ability being built off the foundational principle that sensitivity is necessary for success and growth, patriarchal society is trained to dismiss it. It is for those same reasons—championing sensitivity and openness—that women, LBGTQ people, and emotionally sensitive men tend to proliferate the field and find greater success in wielding psi ability than the stereotypical "manly" man.

Disregarding gender, people who crave consistent results and established outcomes tend to support systems that leave certainty intact. So, they are less likely to be supportive of a mode of thinking that undermines consistency by introducing uncertainty through incorporation of the intangible. Which does not align with the simplest "logical" explanations.

If you hear hooves, you think horses, not zebras. But, psychic ability asks you to think beyond zebras. Is there an intergalactic species that has hooves? Do we know if that is actually the sound of hooves, or could it be something else?

Despite public knowledge of the existence of UFOs, the United States Government has confirmed reports of UFOs flying in our airspace, and the vastness of the universe (and, therefore, its possibilities) is accepted, many *still* refuse to accept alien life as a potential reality.

No matter what you offer skeptics, they will hold to their views. Unless they experience something themselves *and can accept that experience*, they will not entertain such phenomena as psychic ability. They'll say something stupid like, "It's mind-reading"…as if mind-reading isn't an extraordinary phenomenon, especially when compared to psychic sensing.

CHAPTER 3

Pop Goes the Reality Bubble

Inducing Psychic Ability

Before going deeper into psi ability, I have a confession to make. I am not special.

Having a psychic or psi ability is not inherently special. We all have psi ability. It is the willingness to hone that ability over time through diligent practice, to reflect on life's experiences, and to maintain an openness to the unknown that ultimately makes someone special, empowering them to possess and wield their unique psi ability.

Yes, I had a supernatural experience in my kitchen. My mind buzzed with possibilities after. Before the fire, I could *feel* it. I could sense the heat of the fire on my cheeks. I could hear my heart race with fear. I could see it spread and feed before me. All of this percolated inside my mind.

But, that experience did not happen because I'm special or because I have a gift. It happened because I was opening to the possibility of psychic phenomena. The story of Kes unlocked my mind, turning the handle on a door that had long piqued my curiosity but that my legs were too short to reach. Kes's story exposed me to the concept of psychic phenomenon and unconsciously opened my mind to reconceive what is possible. The emergence of my psi ability—the ability that allowed me to witness the fire in my kitchen—was the byproduct of all the experiences in my life leading to that moment, each instance that caused me to consider different possibilities and be open to the infinite set of answers.

It's not just me; many people I know have had their psychic abilities triggered by a single event that prompts them to reconsider the bounds of existence. Just that small sliver of belief in possibilities breaks open a flood of ensuing phenomena. Simply being open and aware of the wealth of possibilities in our existence is one of the easiest ways to trigger a psychic experience.

How I Burst Through the Reality Bubble: The Levels of Reality

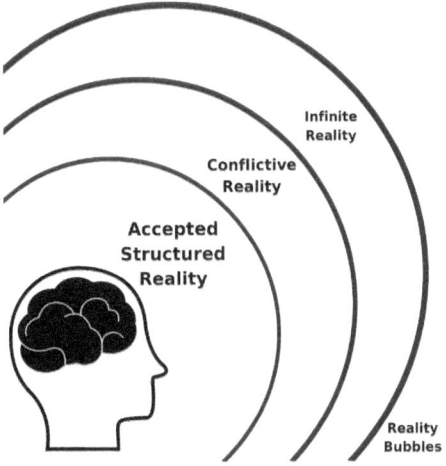

To understand bursting through the reality bubble, we must first understand what we are bursting through. Although I had these profound and unique experiences in my life, I was still predominately existing in Level 1 of reality. I needed to work to experience all that exists at a deeper level.

There are three levels of reality that we can engage with at one time or another. Before my awakening, I could not access deeper levels of reality intentionally. When I would crash into deeper levels, my brain would struggle to understand what I was experiencing. Similarly, most people enmeshed in Level 1 of their life will compartmentalize and try to rationalize any psychic or unusual experience. These aberrations from Level 1 will be logically reasoned away. Or, in the case of a substance-enhanced experience, will be dismissed as a byproduct of too many drugs, too much weed, too much alcohol, sleep deprivation, or things of the like. But these experiences are invitations to engage with the twilight zone, beckoning the conscious into a surreal universe that encourages deeper questions and, as a consequence, deeper understanding.

But first, before we delve deeper, it is important to understand what these levels are and how we interact with them.

Accepted Structured Reality (Level 1) – Let's call this "human experience on autopilot."

Reality Level 1 is the engagement with the established reality and routine operation of our minds, processing what we see and categorizing it into the framework we've been indoctrinated to believe. This rigid state of being abides by societal conventions. It allows us to collaborate and interact with each other on the basis of a shared, universal understanding. In this reality, we are all operating under roughly the same set of accepted rules, shaped by our upbringing, culture, and environment. With our shared understanding in this Reality, we are cued to greet our coworkers, chat excitedly about the upcoming weekend, and reflect fortunately upon great weather.

Level 1 Reality assumes the absence of the supernatural. It proceeds by favoring the replication of past experiences, assuring an existence firmly within what is "known."

Culturally-accepted formalities enable us to operate on autopilot without questioning the nature of our existence. Aberrant events are set aside to fit within the boundaries of what we already know. The concept of coincidence acts as a buffer from confronting deeper levels of reality. What we experience makes sense as it coincides with what we've already experienced. We morph the psyche to fit within this reality structure.

Our experience of reality within Level 1 is surface-deep: it's a superficial awareness based on survival mechanisms and thought patterns, especially surrounding things like health, relationships, and finances.

Conflictive Reality Structure (Level 2) – This is where Level 1 reality cracks, dropping us into Level 2. It is primed by engaging with those difficult questions, and facing the aberrant situations. Level 2 is occupied by paranormal, supernatural, and extraordinary experiences. Simply, Level 2 are phenomena "out of this world."

When the mind becomes opened and primed to see beyond Level 1, the elasticity gained allows for heightened awareness to perceive and contextualize the experiences in Level 2.

One of the most common ways people enter Level 2 is by witnessing phenomena of their own. Additionally, many enter Level 2 by witnessing the abilities of others operating in Level 2 or beyond. Like Kes was to my perception of reality, witnessing the psychic abilities of another can act as a crowbar, freeing the mind from its constraints and shackles to unleash a new plane of being. While the reality encountered by an individual facing a Level 2 opening may not make logical sense and may conflict with their established reality, the experiences within this range of awareness will still encompass familiar categories of phenomena. This means that Level 2 contains an awareness where myths, legends, and ideas like Angels, Spirit Guides, and Santa exist—while not all of these experiences may be "real" in accordance with routine lived experience, these concepts are where Level 2 experiences lie on the reality spectrum; a step beyond the concrete, tangible experiences enveloped by Level 1.

Level 2 is both the familiar and the nearly familiar. It is still impacted by mental filters and each individual's unique lived experience, but it exists beyond the prototypical constraints of the tangible reality of Level 1.

Religious Ideology, Beliefs & The Darker Side of Psychic Experiences

Our daily, busy mind hardly has the room to challenge the concepts that shaped us: our experiences, our beliefs, and our foundational structures. When a supernatural experience comes along, it interacts with the experiences, beliefs, and structures of each person differently, knocking on their door to see if it can find a way inside. Whatever combination of conditioning–experiences, beliefs, and structures–an individual has, they frequently make it far more difficult for a person to understand the depth of their capacities–if they can even recognize their capacities at all!

Whether it be religious ideology, an unwillingness to lose control, or any other mental barrier, the accuracy and awareness of Level 2, Conflictive Reality experiences can be affected by one's conditioning.

Think of having a moment of premonition–the feeling that something bad is about to happen. It starts in the gut, rattling out through the bones, filling the body with dread before forming a concrete thought in the mind: something is coming, and it won't be good. Being uncomfortable or scared can cause a person to dismiss these feelings as irrational, bad, wicked, wrong, evil, the product of a demon or Satan, and so on. Then, when we hear such premonitions from another person, we fear them, so we reject them. Sometimes, it's worse than that. Sometimes, our fears cause us to lash out at the perceived source of our internal conflict, and we can project our hurt and confusion onto the other person. Their nightmare came true, we see, so it must be the work of the devil. It was not the precognition or premonition that acted as a warning. No, the bad was brought by the bearer of the news, we reason. They must be the source. They must be evil.

Those who seek to be in control of everything, too, may fall victim to a similar situation. Control freaks, as I affectionately call them, seek to eradicate the unexpected from their lives. They will not be vulnerable by virtue of surprise or unpreparedness; they will push away those feelings while noting the causes to avoid such experiences in the future. It's clever, certainly. But it is absolutely disastrous for further psychic development and can also set up even more challenging experiences.

Experiences are bound to occur out of the conflictive reality level.

But others with a budding psychic ability want to embrace, evolve, and develop it. Occasionally, they feel as if something is keeping them from experiencing their full potential. In this instance, individuals often hinder their evolution due to a rigid mindset about what psi ability is and isn't. If people believe that the ability is unique, special, and sacred, only reserved for a chosen few, then they've psychologically set up a roadblock in their psyche. A roadblock that has the same effect as the folks who live in fear of loss of control or hold a religious belief about the phenomenon. So, believing that the ability requires huge effort or a significant event to activate is just as devastating to any attempt at building the ability.

Infinite Reality (Level 3) – Unbounded and Unknown

What lies in Level 3 exists independent of mental filters, where one's own beliefs cannot find a foothold to interact with the experience. Level 3 contains an ocean of information that most cannot fully comprehend because of the linear state of being to which we are accustomed. As in, we are so used to thinking from point A to B in Level 1 and can learn how to think from B to Z in Level 2 that it takes a concerted effort to shift from Z to the square root of negative one. We can only comprehend so much of Level 3, even with training and experience, but we are ultimately limited by our corporeal form from understanding it completely.

Imagine Einstein trying to explain his theory of relativity to a small bird. The bird's mind cannot possibly comprehend all of the teachings, especially given its bird brain. The bird would need to evolve into a different form before it could only begin to absorb and meaningfully interact with Einstein's theory. In Level 3, we are the little bird. Our comprehension is limited, by definition.

Level 3 is where the idea of God is situated, where the truth of the source being resides, and where the infinite mind with infinite consciousness expands. Though we may be able to grasp aspects of Level 3 reality, our human perspective largely obscures it from view.

The Floodgates

You're on a road trip. You knew that you should go to the bathroom before leaving, but it just seemed silly. You just went an hour ago, and so you do not need to go now. If you need to go while on the road, you'll hold it until the destination. You sit in the car as your stomach swells with discomfort. You had a couple of sips of water to combat your friend limiting the air conditioning to save gas. Now, you can feel it–the pressure–holding in and fighting what is naturally designed to occur. If you wait too long, it will no longer be up to you. Any laugh, excessive activity, or consumption of fluids will only put more pressure on your system, and you're bound to have an uncomfortable experience if you suddenly release. You'll be right back in the position you were in first grade, surrounded in unintended wetness after an explosion caused by the unconscious mind succumbing to conscious pressure.

This full bladder is an apt metaphor for the sudden experience of psi ability. The fear of loss of control or the blockades of conditioning prevents the system from reconciling what it seeks to do naturally.

The person will hold back on the energy cycling naturally through their system. The system still *needs* a release, but the release is denied. Then, upon the happening of some trauma or any other significant or intense emotional event or thought process, a trigger is hit, and the floodgates open.

I often hear from people who have sudden bursts of psi phenomena, and they don't understand what it is, why it's happening, or what is happening. They do not realize that they've been holding their natural ability back, either because of fear or their conditioning, frequently because of their belief in their faith. In doing so, they are set up for random uncontrolled experiences usually erupting from a place or level of fear and misunderstanding.

We tend to fear what we don't understand, and this kind of occurrence really is quite common. Psi ability is not religious, and it isn't something that is meant to throw your life into chaos. It is a natural phenomenon that can benefit all of us if we simply reframe the way we see it culturally and find a balance in using it to our advantage.

That is what psi is…an advantage in human ability.

Truthfully, I cringe every time I hear my psi ability referred to as a gift, something innate and given from birth. That's not how it happens. That's not how it happens for professional athletes, actors, scientists, lawyers, or any other profession.

No one would dare compare Serena Williams to a casual tennis player because both happen to have natural talent. That's like comparing Linda Ronstadt to someone who only casually and occasionally sings. Linda Ronstadt spent at least six hours a day and decades of control when it came to the development of her skills. Compare her to the casual singer with a good starting point but without the level of ability, control, and skill Linda put herself through with training? No ma'am! Serena's tennis prowess and Linda's vocal abilities are not "gifts." They're skills. They're earned, not given.

Some people may start with a natural talent for psychic ability, come from a line of people with demonstrated psychic ability or grow up in an environment uniquely suited for nurturing psi ability. Even in cases like this, work is required to reach proficiency and sacrifice is required to reach excellence in the craft. It's not a gift. It's the product of years of very hard, deliberate work. I may have been "gifted" with a heightened sensitivity, but, trust me, I've busted my ass to develop my skills to the level they are right now, and I'm busting my ass to get better every day.

Natural ability does nothing if it is not used. Just like becoming Serena starts with playing tennis and becoming Linda starts with singing. The work of developing psi ability starts with the simple act of being open to the idea of psychic phenomena. I've met several natural sensitives who are very capable in their sensing abilities, but without putting in the effort to develop, control, and expand their natural ability, they exist in a limited state. They can't do a reading on the spot or tune into the details of a situation. They see only in the broad strokes of their unrefined talent, often claiming only spontaneous psychic experiences from moments in their life.

With psi ability, you are just as special as I am in that neither of us are particularly special. Just like in life, we're in this together on the same journey to fully harness our psi ability. Like any worthwhile experience, the journey requires work.

Psi Ability Starts Early

Like my psi ability started with my birth, your psi ability started with yours.

The path to my psi awakening began with birth, burgeoned with the curiosity of childhood, and burst when I breached the gates of puberty. With many in my family history seemingly possessing real psi ability, I likely started life with a proclivity towards psi ability, but that is not what got me to this point in my development. Throughout my life, as I wielded my sensitivity as a defense mechanism and a vital tool in my repertoire to avert danger and rebound from disappointment, I was unknowingly deepening my psi potential. Then, as I came to realize what I was doing, my practice became intentional, and I sharpened what was already there.

Children are particularly sensitive to the world around them because they must learn to adapt to situations to increase their chances of survival; they must understand the "norm" to avoid being perceived as other–as unwilling to contribute to the thriving of the larger community. Children, because of their sensitivity and curiosity, are also primed for psi ability, willing to entertain thoughts that are against conventional thinking. How psi ability is nurtured in childhood is greatly influenced by the child's environment. For me, my environment taught me to mute the emergence of my psi abilities.

Animals react before an earthquake or hurricane–they start to gather or migrate, birds tweet, and others bury underground. The animals have a sense of what they're reacting to, primed into them from birth as a means of survival. They lack the barriers of rationality to fight these instincts. They move because they need to survive. Similarly, children lack these barriers. Naturally, this explains why children tend to express more psychic ability and awareness of supernatural phenomena. Their natural ability of awareness, adaptation, and survival is essentially operational at birth. They have yet to be conditioned away from it, and typically no one has guided them in understanding that this is acceptable or a "normal" human mental mechanism. Before being conditioned away from this natural ability, they have the unique experience of sensing things most of us have trained ourselves out of.

After birth, I was a blank slate, free from the imprinting of my family, culture, social norms, values, entertainment, and the bounds of "acceptability." Entering the world, from the moment the doctor said, "It's a boy," the process of conditioning my mind to comply with a conventional worldview and perception of reality began. Conditioning was not a result of malice; rather, it was a result of the adults around me trying to prepare me for survival. Where I grew up purposefully kept me closed off to the possibility of psychic ability. When my sensitivity and curiosity would begin to open the door, the others around me would force it shut.

I remember being a child, having my curiosity actively drummed out of me. Noah had an Ark, they told me. Two animals of each kind were brought into the Ark. But what kind of ramp got them into the Ark? How did he get all the animals to one place? Did he load them onto the Ark after he found them? I sought answers but was met with reproach. How dare I ask questions? This was the truth I was given and the truth I must accept.

And when I became curious about other things, I got the same responses. Don't ask. When I voiced my premonitions, I got the same responses. That's the devil. When I had imaginary friends, at first, it was acceptable. Imaginary friends were normal for young kids–healthy outlets used to process experiences. Occasionally, I would play with my cousin, Jennifer. She was just a few months older than I was. I don't know if she saw them too, but I believe her mind was still flexible enough to accept the entities in my reality. My cousin Monica, a teenager, would watch me and Jennifer sometimes. She, too, accepted and encouraged my play.

I now recognize that these "friends" were early manifestations of my psi development. My mother and Monica offered nurturing strength, embracing me. I wonder if Monica's acceptance stemmed from her veering closer to rejecting our strict Catholic upbringing than any other members of my family. Rumor has it, my aunts–mis tias–would play with tarot cards, indulging in the whimsy and possibility that they represented: a foray into a deeper reality level made safe by a firm avowal that it was just for fun. But if they ever heard that I was engaging with shadow spirits–with my invisible friends–I would have been greeted with an exorcism, not a hug. When my mother delved into her mania, they took her to church. They would rather believe their family member was possessed by evil than consider that the demons she was fighting were of a different creation.

These parental and authoritative figures are the first guiding hands a child has, and the health with which the parent greets their child's curiosity will play a large role in whether their psi ability is nurtured or stomped out. For those blinded by ignorance, fear, or beliefs like religion, the threat of exterminating natural intuition and psychic ability is high. Luckily, I had these pockets of safe spaces where I could explore my own psi ability. I also had plenty of time to myself, leaving me free to engage with *Unsolved Mysteries*, *Sightings*, and other shows that explored phenomena. So, while I saw the potential of psi ability and engaged with it, I never knew that it could be within me, too, and no one in my life would have allowed me to unabashedly pursue it.

Destigmatizing psi ability is crucial to preserve the talents and wonderment of these young children. To maximize their psi potential, the child's exploration needs guidance and patience, facilitating engagement with their potential without fear, shame, or guilt. For that end, many more reality bubbles will need to be popped and the goodness of psi ability made known.

Bursting the Reality Bubble Through Witnessing Real Psychic Ability

I call the established beliefs of an individual as indoctrinated through their childhood, conditioning, and life experiences, their "worldview." Our experiences in childhood shape us into our adult selves, complete with our worldview and its blind spots. The confines of one's worldview dictate their reality bubble. The reality bubble is a safe place where the boundaries are known, and the rules are followed. We seek comfort and retreat to what is known to ease the demands of daily life.

In "developed" countries, our struggle is less about survival and more about accumulating comfort, leading to a stability that begets more stability. We are invincible and safe in our bubbles, so there is no incentive to change the status quo. It's cozy, it works. The saddest part is that *because* our minds are freed from the burden of survival, we have the extra capacity to think beyond our current reality, but few make the choice to engage.

The bubble affirms what we consider to be possible and excludes the impossible. The bubble is big enough to contain all that we know, believe, and support. All of our experiences will fall within the confines of the bubble, existing in harmony with the bounds of our created reality. For those not raised in an environment that encourages expanding boundaries–where supernatural phenomena and extraordinary experiences are dismissed or rationalized– opportunities to express natural psychic ability are minimal, and recognition of such opportunities is unlikely.

But what a budding psychic needs is not to remain in their reality bubble. That reality bubble needs to crack. Hammer to glass. Bone to brick. Smashed. The willingness of an individual to do this independently is rare. To challenge our conditioning is to challenge our essence, risking puncturing our sense of self. That is precisely why witnessing another person unafraid to challenge the status quo of reality through a demonstration of their real psychic activity or by experiencing an electrifying phenomenon can have the rippling effect of awakening dormant psi ability. These are the kinds of events that defy logic and push against an individual's reality bubble, cracking it open to allow for more extraordinary possibilities.

When I think of an electrifying phenomenon that can "shock" an individual out of their reality bubble, I think of being struck by lightning. That's what it feels like. This supernatural force penetrates your skin, reverberating through your muscles and bones, changing the rhythm of your heart, and connecting you to both the sky and the ground in an instant. Or the sudden death of a loved one can crack the reality bubble, the loss of life taking with it a sense of stability. A near-death experience, pushing the body closer to the bounds of reality can also burst the bubble. Any experience that can shift an individual from ordinary to extraordinary–an experience at the extreme of what was previously thought possible–has the potential to shatter the reality bubble.

Sometimes, a crack forms that gradually expands through the advent of more boundary-pushing experiences. Other times, it only takes a single event to push the mind from the safety of the bubble. Sometimes, just seeing a very handsome guy who calls himself a psychic on Instagram Live making incredible connections with strangers can prompt someone to break free from their bubble. And, if you're wondering, I do know a guy that fits this description if you're interested. ☺

But seriously, over the years I've done thousands upon thousands of readings. I've put myself out there and given people opportunities to witness what I can do, live and on the spot. My family and friends have also observed this...and I've noticed a trend. Those folks who witness my abilities start to become more psychic by default and have felt supported in their own experiences by what I've brought forth. Seeing my practice helped to initiate that reality bubble burst, ushering in psi abilities of their own. Truly, it's a domino effect.

I cannot tell you how often people have shared their stories with me. But I can tell you one...

Elle was brought up in a strict Catholic high school, and her worldview was reinforced through Catholic events, services, and people. Although she is still Catholic, her practice is far less structured. As she began to pull away from the confines of the church, parts of her began to open as she asked more questions and probed deeper than ever before.

The openness led to her and her fiancé lying together on the couch one afternoon. They were searching on social media when they found my page. Intrigued, they joined one of the Instagram Live sessions I'd host every Wednesday and Friday. Casual curiosity crescendoed into a craving to connect with her deceased brother. While she hoped for the connection, her fiancé remained steadfastly skeptical.

When I brought her into the live video session, she looked at me intently. I looked back at her, feeling the connection with her and, through that, with her brother. As I peeled back layer after layer of this person she once knew so intimately, she became awestruck. Her eyes widened as I told her how her brother passed. She was terrified and electrified like she could see possibilities once held too tightly to access unroll before her. Her fiancé saw it, too. While he entered a skeptic, he left unable to reconcile what he witnessed with his rational thought.

They continued to talk about the reading that night in bed. Suddenly, all of the lights in the house started flickering. Instantly, they became spooked. They checked the light switch, but it was still in the "on" position. Next, they had to eliminate the possibility that this was a circuit breaker malfunction. A trip down to the box proved that it was not. The lights were back on, so their box of curiosity closed once more.

The lights in the house stopped flickering, but the lights in Elle's head just started. Later that week, she dreamt of a helicopter crash, the propeller spinning as it dropped from the sky. This was an unusual subject for her to dream about, but she cast that thought away. It was just a dream until, a few days later, it wasn't. A helicopter crash featured in the news, but Elle still believed it could have been a coincidence. Still, she remained more curious than ever.

A few weeks later, she was brought up again to participate in my live. The woman I saw was different from the one I'd met before. Like a moth to a flame, energies were drawn to her, and she had *questions*! She told me about a vision she had. As we discussed, I worked to interpret. I told her what I thought happened with one of her relatives. She shook her head, no. Then, she asked her mother about what we uncovered. Her mother confirmed: it was all true. What were the odds? Astronomical.

The next morning, she laid in bed with her fiancé. The two were awoken from their slumber with raucous hip-hop music blaring through a speaker in their bedroom. Despite being silent and nonfunctional for months, the speaker was now working. They went to their neighbors to find a rational explanation for their speaker's sudden resurrection. Nothing. None of them connected to the speaker–none of them could even see the speaker as an option–and none of them could illuminate the source of the sudden noise. Elle and her fiancé returned to their home, both in a daze. The speaker sounded again. Her fiancé was worried, yanking the plug from the wall. She'd never seen her strong, silent type of a man with this unease in his eyes. He was rattled, and his rattle transferred to her. Her Catholic instincts told her that she opened a door to something evil or dark with the readings. Neither of them knew what was happening or why it was happening.

I worked with Elle for a few more weeks. Her initial opening from the first reading unlocked a flood of psychic energy. She tried to remain open, compartmentalize her fear, and plumb the depths of the world around her. Slowly, she acclimated to the discomfort, accepting instead of dissecting her experiences. Elle is still a work in progress. While walking along the consciousness bridge, her receptiveness to psychic information began to cripple her. Overwhelmed by lingering fears and constant communications, she has yet to access her psi potential and break through her blockages to truly engage with her reality. Until she accepts the idea of permanently leaving her current reality, she never will.

CHAPTER 4

Clair Sensing & What They Don't Tell You in Class

Meet Clair.

Claire is *it*.

If I showed you a picture of her, you might roll your eyes. She's petite and effortlessly thin, with naturally thick, dark brown hair. Her beachy waves compliment her California-kissed skin. Her face has light lines of wisdom, complimenting her delicate array of perfectly sprinkled freckles. Oh, and she's a mom. Not just any mom–she's *that* mom–cool and breezy, moving with quiet confidence and electric energy.

There's even more to her...she's incredibly kind and compassionate, empathetic even, in the most difficult situations. Her curiosity greets every situation before permeating its surface, coursing through the subject as she becomes part of its essence.

As a television producer, her days are spent creating immersive experiences through media, translating her curiosity into audience discovery. She educates through her medium, communicating volumes with her work. It engages the senses, invigorating both sight and sound.

I swear, this girl knows everything. When I'm with her, I feel like she is seeing all the way through me, but it doesn't make me invisible–it makes me powerful. If I tried to tell her this, she would simply spin around, smile softly, and say that, from her perspective, she's always with me. She's right, I'd admit, and I have the power to feel her presence at any time.

When I first met Claire, she welcomed me with warmth, and I reciprocated with equal openness. We meshed effortlessly, leaving me with no doubts about anything she chose to share. She was real, and I could feel that energy. I met her without any preconception of who she was, allowing me to accept her as she presented herself. As a result, I now have a beautiful friend who will be with me for the rest of my life.

My Claire reminds me of another Clair. Just like my Claire, this Clair's job is to produce an immersive experience in the medium of the mind. An otherworldly Clair. An ageless Clair. A mythic Clair. And, just like my Claire, this Clair's reputation preceded her.

At first, I'd only heard of this other Clair. Psychic and spiritual friends told me stories about her grandeur and wisdom. Authors lauded her transformative powers. She floated through rooms I'd been in–omnipresent, it seemed, but untouchable. She always seemed just out of reach. When I shared how eager I was for an introduction from a mutual friend, they just told me that it wasn't my time yet. Clair required patience and I needed to be patient.

When the time finally came for me to meet Clair, I confess that I did not even realize it was her. Now, I laugh when I think back on how *thirsty* I was to find the Clair that was described to me in movies, television, books, memoirs, and by other psychics, and friends. I thought she was going to be almost as solid as something I could hold in my hand and as vivid as something I could sketch with a pencil. Her arrival would be unmistakable, accompanied by a delicate but distinct wafting of Dolce & Gabbana Light Blue. When she'd speak, subtitles would cascade from her mouth, ensuring clarity of message. I would be positive it was her, and it would be an unmistakable, magical, and transformative experience.

When she flipped her hair, moonlight would beam, and stars would sprinkle. *That* was the Clair I expected.

It was not the Clair I received.

Clair didn't try to fool me, but by the time I knew what she was, she'd been completely built up into something entirely different. I thought she was complicated and that I'd need to earn the right to bask underneath her. Clair, though, doesn't play those games. She doesn't like gates, walls, passcodes, or keys. Yes, you can sit with her because she's *already* been sitting with you. Clair is French, freakishly misunderstood, and my friend.

Which Clair is Already There?

It's no surprise that Clair is not a real person. The lesson is to treat her like a tangible presence–complex, yet accessible– approaching her with openness instead of expectation.

Clair refers to the psychic impact on the senses. Most people know the main Clair, Clairvoyance. Clairvoyance pairs the French word for clear ("clair") with vision ("voyance") to describe the ability to *see clearly*, which, in the psychic community, usually refers to extrasensory perception. A classic example of clairvoyance is the ability to foresee a future event. My childhood vision of the kitchen fire is an example of clairvoyance–I was able to *see* the fire feed and grow. Clairvoyance allowed me to *perceive* what lay beyond what I could physically *see*.

While clairvoyance is typically used as a broad term, there are other "Clairs" to consider:

Clairaudience ("clear" + "sound") refers to extrasensory hearing, such as hearing the voice of a long-passed loved one while walking by their favorite vase.

Clairsentience ("clear" + "feeling") is being able to pick up on the emotions or energy of an item, place, or person. Imagine standing at a place of deep historical significance, like Harpers Ferry, Virginia, and feeling the deep sadness and defiance of those who perished during John Brown's Rebellion.

Clairalience/clairolfaction ("clear" + "smelling") occurs when picking up a scent despite an absent source, like the smell of Grandma's famous sugar cookies drifting through an open window on the anniversary of her death.

Clairgustance ("clear" + "tasting") refers to experiencing the taste of something without an apparent source, as if you were actually tasting Grandma's cookies, instead of smelling them.

Claircognizance ("clear" + "awareness") is a curious clair, signifying the ability to know, without prior knowledge, logic, or sensory input, facts about another person, situation, or event. An example from my life occurred at the beginning of the COVID-19 pandemic. I intuitively knew how long it would take for a vaccine to be developed, that it would be based on mRNA, and that three brands would be involved in the initial round of vaccinations—despite having almost no prior knowledge about pharmaceuticals, vaccines, or the average timeline for bringing a new medication to market.

Clairtangency ("clear" + "touching") is best described as being able to touch something and gather information from that object, be it a person, place, or thing. One of the best examples of clairtangency is when a psychic can touch the object of a missing person, like a sock or a shoe they left behind, and extract details about their whereabouts.

Clearly, clairs are a big deal and are powerful resources in the work of a psychic. These are only *some* of the crew, and multiple clairs can be experienced at once. No wonder I was so nervous!

Why Can't I Find Her?

Understanding that clair is important to psychic ability is easy; much harder is separating what clair "is" from what we have been told. I love Raven Symone, but *That's So Raven* is a great example of the high expectations people hold for clairvoyance. For the uninitiated, in *That's So Raven*, Raven Symone plays "Raven," an ordinary high schooler navigating the challenges of school, friendships, and family while also experiencing unsolicited visions of the future. Raven can't control the content or timing of her visions. When they come, she is left frozen in the middle of whatever she's doing, unable to interrupt the autoplay of the vision until it finishes. As the audience, we know we're entering a vision when the camera zooms into Raven's eye, allowing us to watch the vision unfold as clearly as the surrounding scene. The content of the vision is clear, but the context is left to Raven's interpretation, usually leading to her devising a plan to change the future. The theme song is a bop, too: "That's So Raven! It's the future I can see. That's So Raven! It's so mysterious to me."

For the longest time, I thought that's what Clairvoyance looked like–a pop-up ad on autoplay in my head–vivid and unambiguous in content, separate from my passing thoughts and memory. For clairalience, if I didn't feel like the flower was beneath my nose and the only thing I could smell, then it couldn't be Clair. Clairaudience was a bell ringing in my ears completely indistinguishable from an actual bell less than a yard away. It wasn't until I was on the eve of founding my own practice that I began to understand the wide range of ways that Clair could work to transmit information psychically. Nothing–not other psychics, development books, or media– had truly prepared me for what I would actually experience with Clair, so getting Clair "right" was a process.

As I've said before, you do not need to be "special" to be psychic, and you do not need to have "powers" to engage with the clairs.

Ever had a "gut feeling" that something was going to happen? Hello, claircognizance! You knew without having a reason for knowing–the knowledge came to you, and then, you *knew*. Murky, sure, but practice helps mop up some of the murk.

Visions like Raven's are certainly possible, and some people are energetically sensitive enough to have such vivid and direct physical experiences of their perceptions. However, most of the psychics I've met do not engage with their psychic senses this way. Moreover, every individual interacts with the clairs in different ways, typically leading to every psychic having a favorite. Noreen Rainier, famed psychic detective, is closest with clairtangency. In the b-roll for her episodes of *Psychic Investigators*, she is visibly clutching objects, inspecting their edges with her eyes sealed tightly, letting the items speak to her through their grooves. From the information in her hands, an entire scene unfolds, and everything becomes *clear* to her. Once I realized that Clair works differently for each person, it changed the way I used my abilities and helped me focus on what I was actually capable of sensing.

Before we continue dancing with Clair, let's sit down for a second and properly introduce ourselves to her.

Let's use that same red apple from Chapter 2.

- You can close your eyes for a few seconds and then rejoin me here if that makes it easier.
- Open your eyes again to read this. Take a few moments to describe that apple. What is the apple doing? Where is the apple? How does the apple look? Stop.
- Close your eyes again as you think "What does that apple mean to you?" Just sit for a few seconds thinking about what the apple means to you.

Thank you for participating! I hope you're not hungry, now. We have a little more business to take care of before the next section.

The red apple.

Memory is the easiest way to gain extrasensory information. From birth, we have been adding to our internal library of meaning. From a young age, we were taught to associate things with meaning, helping us produce a very robust, untapped potential when dealing with our psychic senses. Most of us associate objects or ideas with some sort of memory. When I ask you to think about a red apple and tell me what it means, your memory activates, and your mind reaches for an association. Now, there is an idea or thought developing context where there previously was nothing, infusing itself with (depending on how old you are) decades of meaning. It reveals far more than what we initially imparted to it.

I hear "red apple," and my mind begins to swirl. A green, lumpy, misshapen nose appears in the cold, reflective glass of an ornately gold-rimmed mirror. Eyes slowly come into focus–each large, circular, and white with a large black pupil suspended within. The apple is rotating, an unidentified light source from above casting a shiny ring around its upper edges, colors darkening as they are pulled toward the center where a thick, blunt stem reaches upwards from a crevice. My red apple belongs to the Evil Queen and will be sent to sweet Snow White's unsuspecting lips, causing her to fall into a deep, painless sleep.

But you may hear "red apple" and think of another instance of innocence corrupted. Eve's fear as she realizes that the serpent sold her a ticket out of her home, ashamed for succumbing to the evil of curiosity. Or maybe, you have a positive association with corrupted innocence and apples, imagining the warmth of a nice, spiked apple cider on a crisp Thanksgiving afternoon–a reward for pretending to want to watch six hours of football in a row. Maybe you just imagined apple pie, got hungry, put the book down, and are now resuming reading with a few crumbs still gracing your face. Sure, the pie wasn't from the bakery down the street from your childhood home, but it tasted like they added some caramel and cinnamon to your nostalgia.

A Brief History of Clair: Was She Always There?

The clairs have been around for as long as humanity. Details of prophecies, oracles, and visions litter ancient religious texts and literature–from the Oracle of Delphi to Nostradamus. Jainism, one of the oldest religions still practiced today, teaches that knowledge takes five different forms, one of them *"Avadhi Jnana,"* or clairvoyance.[1] Every prophecy in the Bible is a form of clairvoyance– an individual's assertion in the present about something that will occur in the future.

The concept of "Clair" began to seep into the mainstream as something separate and apart from prophecies, oracles, and visions during the Spiritualism Movement of the 19th Century. Taking place first in North America before spreading to England and Europe, Spiritualism's growth can be traced, at least in part, to society's growing urbanization and disenchantment with the human condition in an increasingly modern society marked by industrialization and technological advancement.[2] As society industrialized and urban centers grew, daily tasks shifted from meaningful to menial, and living conditions for the working class went from spacious to squalid. Collectively, people became curious about whether there was, in fact, "more" to life, and how that "more" could be uncovered.

Spiritualism encouraged a new way of perceiving the world–it sought understanding beyond the spheres of reality. Unsurprisingly, this new way of thinking garnered the interest of many prominent

---

[1] https://www.wisdomlib.org/definition/avadhijnana

[2] https://www.bowdoin.edu/news/2018/01/victorian-spiritualism-when-ghosts-and-objects-collide.html

figures. Sir Arthur Conan Doyle, author of *Sherlock Holmes*, was a prominent spiritualist, serving as the President of the British College of Psychic Science and authoring *The History of Spiritualism*.[3] He called the Spiritualist movement "the most important in the history of the world since the Christ episode."[4] Inventor Thomas Edison made efforts to develop a "spirit phone" that would be able to record the voices of the deceased in the years before his 1931 death.[5] Sigmund Freud, father of Psychoanalysis, contributed an essay on subconscious thought to the 1912 edition of the Society for Psychical Research's journal.[6] Freud likely would have engaged in more psychical research had he not feared that steering his work more firmly into parapsychology would alienate the members of the public just beginning to accept psychoanalysis.[7][8]

---

[3]

https://archive.org/details/historyofspiritu015638mbp/page/n1/mode/1up

[4] https://gutenberg.net.au/ebooks03/0301051h.html

[5] https://www.forbes.com/sites/kristintablang/2019/10/25/thomas-edison-bc-forbes-mystery-spirit-phone/

https://web.archive.org/web/20191025123851/https://www.forbes.com/sites/kristintablang/2019/10/25/thomas-edison-bc-forbes-mystery-spirit-phone/

[6] https://muse.jhu.edu/article/156

[7] In a 1921 letter, Freud wrote: "I am not one of those who dismiss a priori the study of so-called occult psychic phenomena as unscientific, discreditable or even as dangerous. If I were at the beginning rather than at the end of a scientific career, as I am today, I might possibly choose just this field of research, in spite of all difficulties." https://daily.jstor.org/when-psychoanalysts-believed-in-magic/

[8] His official biographer, Ernest Jones, worked to persuade Freud not to publish his paper on Psycho-Analysis and Telepathy, among others. Jones, Ernest, *The Life and Work of Sigmund Freud*, 391-394. https://archive.org/details/dli.ernet.138917/page/395/mode/2up

Spiritualism, in embracing openness of thought, found itself actively engaged in challenging existing societal constructs. Spiritualists were early and vocal supporters of deviations from societal norms, including supporting the abolition of slavery and women's suffrage.[9] Many women were members of the movement and found themselves in positions of leadership.[10] Although Spiritualism's rise coincided with the rise of detractors and skeptics, nothing could stop interest in the field that would later be coined parapsychology. Today, both the British College of Psychic Science and the Society for Psychical Research are still functioning organizations, spreading peer-reviewed work and increasing awareness and education.

The Kaleidoscopic Memory of Clair

This very brief history of the Clairs serves two points: (1) the Clairs have been embedded in our societies across different cultures and eras and (2) the recognition of the Clairs is not entirely foreign to some scientists. While skeptics advocate for a clear separation between the Clairs and mainstream scientific thought, this deep connection between the self and the Clairs warrants exploration,

---

[9] "Apart from a quorum of Universalists and a few Unitarians, its leadership was almost entirely lay, often women in a time when their sex had very slim opportunities to exercise spiritual leadership in most established denominations. It was largely a proletarian religious movement in significant alliance with that class's new literacy and sense of a power to make itself heard and, moreover, to remake the world. Early Spiritualism therefore perceived itself as a voice of the 'progressive' movements of the time." Robert Ellwood, How New is the New Age, in Perspectives on the New Age, ed James R. Lewis, J. Gordon Melton, 1992

[10]

https://www.bbc.co.uk/religion/religions/spiritualism/history/history.sht
ml

particularly at the intersection of the Clairs and cognitive psychology.

Let me explain.

Recall the red apple. To recall the apple is to recall a memory and the associations related to the memory. In cognitive psychology terms, my recognition memory is activated. Seeing the apple tells my brain to gather all of the information I have stored away related to it–so I *recognize* the apple and am aware of its meaning.

Recognition memory is a crucial part of episodic memory. Episodic memory involves the ability to recall specific events and their associated details. When an object triggers a memory, neural pathways associated with that memory activate, which can lead to the retrieval of related information and experiences. Essentially, seeing the object activates pathways formed by the memories associated with it. When we see the object again, the same pathways light up, allowing the mind to dance along them and retrieve the associated memories. Part of the reason why memory can be imperfect is that the pathways change over time, like when the flow of the river changes its banks. When a pathway is not accessed for an extended period, it can fade away or require significant effort to reactivate. Accessing information frequently deepens the pathway, making it harder to fade away.

Recognition memory typically takes two forms: item recognition and source recognition.

Through item recognition, I may recognize or remember specific items or objects, such as recognizing a familiar face, a previously seen word, or a particular object. I see red fruit with a small stem shaped a bit like a fist, and I recognize that it is an apple.

Through source recognition, I can recall the context (or source) of an item, recognizing that I've encountered it before, as well as where and when that encounter took place. Source information can include the temporal source (when the item was encountered), spatial source (where the item was encountered), social source (who provided the item), and task context (the context in which an item was presented). I see an apple, and I recall when I learned about all the different types of apples in second grade, I remember the crispness of the last apple I ate, I replay the face of my second grade teacher, and I relate the apple to the context of eating and the act of growing food.

With recognition memory activated, item and source recognition provides the context for the object. I may even hit a psychological trigger, meaning a stimulus or event that can evoke a strong emotional or psychological response in an individual. These triggers are typically associated with past experiences, memories, or traumas and can cause an immediate and often involuntary reaction. Perhaps the item I recall is strongly linked to a person, conjuring up "object-person associations," or the cognitive process by which individuals link a specific object with a particular person based on their shared experiences, interactions, or memories. Maybe I see an apple, and I think of my mom because we would bake apple pie every Fourth of July. Then I think about my cousins because we would bring the pie to our family celebration. Finally, I would think about tasting the sweet, tanginess of the pie as we launched mostly legal fireworks into the street on a clear, summer night.

In sum, the experience of the memory may include a tapestry of attributes including various sounds, smells, tastes, and feelings.

The red apple is not just a red apple. It is the apple that makes the pie I shared with my cousins. Then, it is something that twists and spins in the mirror, keeping me in my childhood memories while proceeding down a different pathway. I find myself in a state of tension as I fear its poisoned nature's effect on the hapless Snow White, so innocent and unassuming, just like me. The apple is not only influenced by the past, it is influenced by the present, including the context under which the recall is made. It is also influenced by Clair, who helps to synthesize the multiple dimensions of experiential data, adding new details to the recalled object.

Close the Books – A Lesson in Finding Clair

Each recall of this memory is a form of psychic sensing and a simple way to receive information. Psychic sensing is not just the physical manifestation of what is experienced through these senses; it is also the recall of past sensory perceptions occurring throughout a psychic's life.

Many times, I will begin a class full of eager students as hungry as I was to find Clair. They, too, imagine her to be this unattainable ideal experienced in stark relief. Developmental courses can contribute to this feeling of unattainability by demanding that one start from a blank space, formulating content from a void instead of using the mind's preexisting memories as essential building materials. My students will be shocked when I let them in on a little secret: there is no need to start from a blank slate. Memory recall–starting with the apple instead of with nothingness–is the easiest way to gain details and information from clients during readings. Instead of waiting for something to appear in my brain, I allow my mind to use what it already possesses–the memories therein–and move from there. Newbie psychics that reject the advantages of their mind in favor of an absolutist approach can find themselves set back years in training. By waiting around to have that direct physical experience, they miss out on the valuable insights and experiences they already possess. Once the reality of how Clair operates is accepted, the student can shift easily into a more effective mode of operating and perceiving.

I once welcomed a new student to train with me. She'd primed herself with many developmental courses before our meeting and had directly trained with others in the industry. When working with her, I noticed she was still expecting to have very direct experiences and dismissed what her mind was continuously trying to give her from memory recall. Her inability to have the archetypal Clair experience left her wondering if she was blocked or, worse, just "really bad at being psychic." After allowing herself to experiment with her psychic potential, including by using memory recall, she uncovered new depths of psychic abilities. Whereas she once believed claircognizance was her only psychic ability, she now regularly taps into extrasensory information and is en route to discovering her true potential. As a teacher, it is a treat for me to continue to watch her embrace of concepts and expansions of potential.

Memory recall does not need to be an "apples-to-apples" comparison. During one client reading, I was asked by a client if she and her husband would stay together. While tuning into her, the memory of my cousin Nick and his wife floats to the front. I've known them for many years, but the memories that fly forward are of a specific type. These memories underscore how the couple remained together out of habit and comfort, creating something that works for them. Considering the memories at the forefront, I began interpretation. I predicted that the client and her husband were going to have the same sort of path in their relationship. They'll stay together because of habits and because their partner is a source of comfort, but the relationship will require work to be healthy and functional. When the image of Nick and his wife emerged, I embraced what it could mean in terms of my client, welcoming it to the table as a communication from my psychic senses.

To reject this offering from my senses would be silly at best and counterproductive at worst. Instructors who expect new psychics to ignore the offerings from their mind in favor of clearing space for something "brand new" or "special" are, in my opinion, either trying to milk money for themselves or have bought into the misinformation. Don't waste your money!

One of the reasons why I love talking about how the mind works in our "normal" reality perception versus extrasensory perception is because the concepts are intimately connected. Extrasensory perception speaks *your* unique language so that *you* can understand, using what is in your mind to create a new image. While our perception is influenced by memories formed through "normal" perception, it is also influenced by extrasensory perception, whether consciously or unconsciously.

How is this possible?

See, our minds are not our own. Each one has a special combination of factors to form its unique language, but part of that language is acquired externally. Our minds are created from our environments, from our experiences, and our degree of openness. Rejecting what our minds present to us also means dismissing the insights offered by forces both within and beyond the mind.

That is why it is so dangerous for these instructors to expect an individual to start from a blank slate during a reading. Doing so urges misinterpretation, forcing things that may be important to disappear. Manipulated results are inaccurate results. As the mind builds images for us, we must accept what we perceive. Be curious!

A closed mind opens no doors.

CHAPTER 5

Telepathy or Random Memory?

Imagine an entire orchestra playing. Make it Beethoven's Symphony No. 5 in C Minor. You know, the one that starts with "da da da duuum." It opens with violas, cellos, and double basses before the rest of the orchestra joins in, swelling into a rich tapestry of different families of instruments that play on the opening theme. Each instrument frantically tries to get its notes out, unconcerned about what the others are doing. To the ear, however, the instruments are working together to create a single work–a symphony.

Telepathy builds in the same way–telepathy is a symphony. Each instrument is unique, producing its own timbre and quality, informed by characteristics like age, experience of player, and location. Our consciousness is that instrument, constantly playing a tune, vibrating within our heads. Telepathy occurs when another instrument joins in, bringing in its distinct melodic components. The instruments engage in conversation, and every new instrument layers deeper meaning into the mix. Harmonization. Discord.

Clairvoyance, clairalience, and the other "clairs" are simply terms to describe the transmission of information to the mind through the senses. It is all about our mind's relationship with the clair sense. Telepathy, on the other hand, is about the mind receiving information from other minds–it is about the relationship between people. With Clair, I am the trigger–I start the process of receiving, dissecting, and interpreting Clair's information. But with telepathy, it is not triggered by the self. It is triggered either by the unconscious mind or by an external trigger.

Popular depictions of telepathy typically feature smooth edges: a zoom-in on someone's forehead, their eyebrows moving dramatically as their internal narrative plays before cutting to the intended recipient of their message, eyebrows raised indicating receipt before returning to voiceover to transmit a message of their own. Telepathy: it's just like speaking, but it's wireless *and* Bluetooth-free!

Unlike sending a text message or receiving a phone call, telepathy is seldom so explicit. Telepathic communication is not a complete language spoken between minds. While each mind may possess the same shared symbols, each mind communicates with its own syntax, diction, or idiosyncrasy, creating a unique language that necessitates *translation* by the receiver if the message is to be received with any accuracy. Like any other wireless carrier, telepathic reception does not come free. It still requires work to send and receive intentionally and with accuracy.

Telepathic Psychology 101

Let's go back to Daddy Freud. As his career progressed, he became more open to the idea of telepathy or "thought transference." In his essay *Psycho-Analysis and Telepathy*, he described a telepathic transference where a fortune teller "diverted her psychical forces" to absorb those of her client, "allowing herself to become accessible to the effects upon her" from her client's thoughts.[11] The result was the wish of one person finding "conscious expression in a slightly

---

[11] https://www.valas.fr/IMG/pdf/Freud_Complete_Works.pdf pp. 3869

disguised form" in the second person.[12],[13] He was especially interested in the relationship between dreams and telepathy, believing the unconscious mind was primed to represent the thoughts or feelings of another.[14]

Carl Jung, a colleague of Freud, also believed in telepathic communication. His work focused on a concept called the "collective unconscious," a shared psychic heritage among all individuals. The collective unconscious contains universal experiences, memories, and symbols that have accumulated throughout human evolution. It manifests in the form of archetypes common across different cultures. The result is a universal base language embedded in each unconscious mind, uniting every individual unconscious mind through the common language.

For example, the "Wise Old Man" archetype exists in many cultures separated by continents, languages, and times: Taoism's Lao Tzu, Greco-Roman mythology's Jupiter/Zeus, the Arthurian Legend Merlin, Ghana Ashanti's Anansi the Spider, and variations of Grandfather Fire among some Native American cultures. Even when you read "Wise Old Man," a specific image popped into your head, and you had a reference point without the provided additional context. The "Wise Old Man" exists within the collective unconscious, and your interpretation of it is influenced by your personal experiences.

---

[12] *Id.*

[13] "What lies between these two mental acts may easily be a physical process into which the mental one is transformed at one end and is transformed back once more into the same mental one at the other end." *New Introductory Lectures on Psycho-Analysis* (p 4664 https://www.valas.fr/IMG/pdf/Freud_Complete_Works.pdf)

[14] Dreams and Telepathy, 1922.

Expanding the concept of the collective unconscious leads to telepathy, or the communication of elements shared between two or more minds, whether conscious or unconscious, in the absence of verbalization. In other words, telepathy is energy and thought transference from one "mind" to another. Telepathy works because our minds are not our own: they operate within the collective unconscious, carrying much more than we can ever truly know.

It is easiest to conceptualize the collective unconscious as a symphony occurring at a very high level, with untold complexity and unlimited duration. Returning to the idea of our mind as an instrument that produces the "tune" of our consciousness, our instruments do not play in isolation. When thoughts race across our minds, our instrument is playing a tune. As we play, the tune enters and intermingles with other tunes in the collective unconscious. But a symphony needs an orchestra, and an orchestra is composed of a variety of instrument groups that play together to create a specific group of sounds. Our innermost circle is our instrument section–the soprano woodwinds playing the major chord progression arranged in counterpoint–and our constant interplay with these members fosters easier telecommunication. But still, we are all connected (just some more closely connected than others).

"I Was Just Thinking About You!"

One of my first memories of telepathy occurred at a Citgo Gas Station–an unremarkable place for a remarkable experience. It was a sticky day, but time was breezing by because I was with my tia. Tia Melba. Tia Melba was eccentric. The color of her kinky, curly ringlets would change with her mood, sometimes as often as the seasons. She was the risk-taker of her siblings–the one that set trends, listened to her own compass and spoke her mind fearlessly. Lime green socks with black pumps? If Tia Melba was wearing it, then it was right! To this day, I still have a lock of her hair (a blonde one, of course).

In the car that day, however, I saw shock flick across Tia Melba's face. She'd reapplied the gas cap and hung up the hose, angled around the edges of her faded sedan, and shut the driver door. She was talking about something as she clicked the seatbelt in the driver's seat. Her words were interrupted by a gasp, Tia Melba's eyes grew wide as her mouth dropped open. Color drained from her face like she'd seen a ghost. I followed her gaze to a point fixed ahead. The point was a man. A man? Aunt Melba's head turned slowly, each motion matching his footsteps. A man now standing at the driver's side window. She rolled down her window. "Son of a bitch!" Laughter erupted from her deepest belly, replacing the air's tension with relief. "You scared the hell out of me! I was just thinking about you!"

See, Aunt Melba had *just* been thinking about this man. He was a friend of her husband's, and she hadn't heard from him in a while. She knew his home situation was unstable, and he was between places. She wondered how he was doing and if he'd found his footing. When her eyes found him, she thought she'd made him appear. She wasn't even sure he was real until his face changed in response to her laugh. The laugh was Tia Melba hanging up the telepathic phone to speak in person.

Almost everyone has had the experience of thinking about a person when that person's name begins to light up their phone. Upon answering, you exclaimed, "I was *just* thinking about you!" How uncanny for your thought to be interrupted by the subject of your thought! What a strange coincidence! When they popped into your head, they were *in* the process of reaching out to you. A beautiful cosmic connection and a very basic example of telepathy.

Telepathic communications occur most frequently between those with a close bond—our families, friends, and lovers—because the amount of time we spend with those people creates a shared space, or overlapping consciousness, between us. This exists *in addition* to the collective unconscious mind plane already shared. So, our telepathic communication with that person can be triggered by a wide range of things, including the invocation of an experience shared by both parties.

Take the following story of a dear friend:

One lazy mid-April Saturday, Rhonda begins to stir, feeling like this may be the time to finally tackle the task of cleaning out her closet. Over the years, she's gained and lost weight as items have gone in and out of style. We're not talking "flapper" dresses, but Rhonda spots a pair of tye-dyed ultra-low rise skinny jeans, and she knows they've got to go. About an hour later, half her hangers are empty, and a heartily growing pile of last season's finest sits behind her. After glancing over her shoulder at the pile, the chunky stripe of a Pom Pom scarf catches her eye. Irma. That was a matching scarf she bought with Irma on their 2009 trip to New York. It was supposed to be boho chic, Rhonda giggles to herself. She hadn't spoken to Irma for a few weeks now, not that that was unusual in their advancing age. Rhonda decided she was going to call Irma…right after finishing with her closet.

Meanwhile, Irma found herself working on a Saturday, again. The end-of-quarter duties continued to mount as she felt increasingly isolated from her humanity. Amidst stressing about stressing, her stomach began to burble, quite an unusual situation since Irma's stress levels kept her practically unable to eat. She's craving…a bagel…no, a GOOD bagel…like the one she had with Rhonda at W 112th St. & Broadway in February 2009. Now *that* was a good bagel made better by the presence of a great friend. Although she knows she is supposed to be checking the next row of the spreadsheet in front of her, she's feeling gripped by something strange. The next numbers her fingers type render a phone line trilling. Rhonda answers, "I was *just* thinking of you!"

Irma responded, "What a coincidence!" But, what Irma deemed a coincidence was actually telepathic communication and thought transference.

Let's break down the sequence of events. from an energetic perspective. This way, you'll have a clearer understanding of how this telepathic event happened.

(1) Rhonda's memory recall was triggered by unearthing the faux boho scarf while cleaning her closet.

(2) The scarf is strongly associated with Irma, as they bought the scarves together, resulting in her mind making a person-object association.

(3) The person-object association conjures feelings of longing and attachment to Irma.

(4) Rhonda resolves to call Irma to contend with her feelings of attachment and longing.

After experiencing thoughts 1 and 2, a feeling (3) resulted, leading to the forming of an intent (4). When a thought-feeling-intent chain manifests within a person's being, the **energy transference charge** becomes activated. Almost like an electric zap, a signal immediately goes out to connect to Irma's mental system.

When Irma's mind receives the charge, it starts processing the energy "data" it is receiving, making the mind unconsciously aware of what Rhonda is doing. The "data" is not perfectly translated by Irma's mind–it does not have the Rhondetta Stone to translate perfectly from Rhonda to Irma–but her mind can process the **easiest reference to the specific energy** "data" delivered. Irma may not be able to interpret, "I was cleaning out my closet, saw this scarf from our New York trip, and I missed you." Irma may interpret a highlight of their time together, settling on her trip-making bagel, causing her to think about food and become hungry for the bagel they shared. As the trip moves to the forefront of Irma's mind, she thinks of Rhonda and is compelled to reach out.

Neither one of them was aware that they just transferred energy amongst themselves, and so, they assumed the coincidence was of no consequence.

Here's another example of telepathic communication which may or may not (…okay, "may") be taken from my own life:

You're at home watching television while your partner graciously goes out to do the grocery shopping. Through the magic of marketing, you've managed to make it through the ad break with only one commercial stuck in your head. A new flavor of Doritos? It's "cool ranch" but also "flaming hot"? It's cool and flaming at the same time? Your curiosity is piqued, and you start to crave a spicy-cool crunch. Remembering that you also love human beings that are not edible, delicious, fried chips featuring a heavenly, oxymoronic pairing of heat and tang, you recall that your partner is currently at the grocery store. You briefly ponder asking them to pick it up, even though you've been perfect throughout "no-snack November," but the show is starting again, and you really don't want to be set back on your goals, so you say nothing.

Two and a half episodes later, your partner comes home with the goodies. As they empty their bag on the kitchen table, you notice a misfit. It almost seems like a mirage. Flaming. Hot. Cool. Ranch. Doritos. They *are* real. You wonder if the living room is bugged and whether he heard you have an almost Homer-Simpson-Mmm-Donuts response to a Dorito. You briefly tense. "Hey, boo, so what's with the Doritos?" You inquire. "I just had this weird craving in the store, and they seemed interesting. I didn't want to mess up your diet, so I just snagged a small bag. I'm sure I could eat the whole thing in, like, six bites if you don't want to mess up your diet.

But in case you wanted to try one or three, we can get our fix and then pretend like this never happened."

This kind of telepathic ping pong is very common among people with an intense interpersonal bond, like twins or romantic partners. When individuals are connected in multiple ways, like sharing the same activity and space while being interpersonally close to each other and amassing numerous shared experiences, it becomes much easier to transfer energy back and forth. Suddenly, you'll remark a thought as the other person is uttering the same thing. The more intense a bond, the more our experiences synchronize, and the more frequently energy transfer occurs. I cannot tell you how often a client thinks their jackass of an ex is their soulmate or twin flame because of this formed psychic link between the two of them. No, ma'am. That dream and their coincidental text the next day does not mean you should take their toxic ass back.

What Does "Woof" Mean?

So many people lament being unable to understand their pets. They look at their adorable "best friend" and wonder, "Does Donatella the Poodle know what I'm saying?" If she could speak our language, she'd shake her head in disappointment and say, "Really? And after everything I do for you! I don't give you my toys for my own health. Psh." Then, she'd roll over for a belly rub, asking for you to "make it right." She is a diva, after all, just like you raised her.

But, if you listen closely, you can know what your animal is thinking. Just like a good friend, having a close relationship with an animal creates ample opportunities for energy transfers through shared experiences and mutual understanding. We may not speak the same language, but we have created a vocabulary of symbols approximating a "pack" language. It's how we know our pet is sad, even if they are not crying. We can feel their anxiety and understand their intentions. This relationship is primitive and born out of evolution. As the species learned to depend on each other, the ability to communicate had to strengthen for the sake of survival.

In 2000, Rupert Sheldrake and Pamela Smart undertook a very important question: can we communicate telepathically with our pets? They became intrigued by claims of dog owners that their pets seemed to know when they were about to come home. Maybe it was that they could smell their humans or knew their routine; maybe they received cues from other people in the home; maybe it was chance. So, they conducted an experiment where they videotaped Jaytee, Pamela's dog, in different environments to see if Jaytee would go into an anticipatory state (wait by the window) before the owner would return home. Using over 100 observations, they found that Jaytee would go to the window 55% of the time during the first 10 minutes of the owner's ride home and 23% of the time in the 10 minutes before the owner actually arrived home. These statistically significant results indicate that the dog's level of anticipation surpasses simple reactions to routine or environmental cues, suggesting a more complex form of awareness or communication. It wasn't just a response to routine. It was something deeper.[15]

Ask anyone you know with a pet camera, and I'm sure they will confirm this telepathic connection. My friend has a camera to watch her pet. For the most part, she and her dog are inseparable. When they are apart, though, she can sense when he is most in need of contact. She will say what her dog is doing, open her camera app, and the dog will be doing that same thing. For his part, he senses her emotions. When she's had a tough day, the dog immediately puts his paw on her chest, nuzzling in for a hug. In a very real way,

---

[15]https://www.sheldrake.org/research/animal-powers/a-dog-that-seems-to-know-when-his-owner-is-coming-home-videotaped-experiments-and-observations

they are best friends, so it is not surprising that they transfer energy as dear friends would.

Strangers In Name, Only

We send and receive telepathic signals all the time, often without realizing it. When I worked at Starbucks, I would see hundreds of orders a day. Hundreds of orders means hundreds of different drinks, right? I call this the "same wave" phenomenon. On any day, there would undoubtedly be coincidental groupings of the same order at the same time. I would be at the drive-thru window: "Grande White Mocha, non-fat milk." I walk inside and hear from a person at the register, "Venti White Mocha, non-fat milk." A mobile order comes in: "Grande White Mocha, 1 pump sugar-free Vanilla, non-fat milk." The first time I actively noticed this, I thought, "Seems like basic is contagious." But after I saw it the first time, I couldn't *stop* seeing it. These groupings of "same wave" ordering would happen *all the time* regardless of promotional tie-ins or pop culture events. People were energetically receiving the same fundamental thought and then framing it through their individualized perspectives. Whether meaning to or not, they were all on the same wave, just different surfboards.

The "Same Wave" effect is just another way to describe dipping into the collective unconscious. While the most likely recipient of an energy transfer is an emotionally close person, energy transfer can occur between strangers. We just need to be riding the same wave, be it thinking about the same thing, participating in the same activity, or existing in the same space. It is just a little sad to think that we could be on the same wave as someone yet never know it: those White Mochanistas will never know their kinship!

To demonstrate the telepathic connection between strangers, Thommy Ten and Amalie van Tass conducted a demonstration in a packed auditorium during a TedX conference in Vienna, Austria.

They first went up to a random woman in the audience and asked her to raise her left hand. As abruptly as she cooperated, they were on to another audience member, asking him to raise his left hand. After he did, they asked him about his ideal vacation place. Barcelona, he responded. Amalie noted his response, "Barcelona," she repeated in a Castilian accent.

Next, Thommy approached another random member in the audience who they would want to randomly appear in front of them. The woman answered "Brad Pitt," of course. This continued for the next couple of minutes–asking a random member of the audience a seemingly unrelated question.

Eventually, the hosts brought the "Brad Pitt" woman and "Barcelona" man to the stage. These were not volunteers–just audience members who responded once a microphone was shoved in front of them.

"Brad Pitt" and "Barcelona" were strangers to each other. As they stood across from each other on the stage, Amalie led them in an exercise. "Brad" and "Barcelona" inhaled and exhaled together, seemingly calming their nerves. Amalie asked them to look into each other's eyes. They did. Amalie then instructed them to raise their hand at the sound of a clap. CLAP. Like a mirror, their hands raised.

Then, "Brad Pitt" and "Barcelona" were taken to different parts of the stage and seated on their stools. Positioned toward the audience and in parallel with each other. "Brad Pitt" crossed her legs while "Barcelona" sat with his hands on his knees and legs ajar.

Thommy walked over to "Brad Pitt" and blindfolded her. Thommy told "Brad Pitt" that he'd tap her on the shoulder, and she should raise her left arm into the air after feeling the tap. Surely enough, he tapped, and her hand went up. Amalie directed "Barcelona" to do the same thing–raise his arm once he felt Amalie's touch. Amalie touched him, and his hand went up.

Thommy and Amalie left "Barcelona" and "Brad Pitt" on their stools and crossed to the center of the stage. Holding up the fingers used for the shoulder taps, Thommy and Amalie briefly touched their fingers together. After a few beats, they returned to the side of "Brad Pitt" and "Barcelona," respectively.

Amalie tapped "Barcelona" on the shoulder. His hand went up. Across the stage, a still-blindfolded "Brad Pitt" moved in unison with "Barcelona" despite not being tapped. Amalie continued to tap "Barcelona's" shoulder, yet both "Barcelona" and "Brad Pitt" responded. The connection between these strangers became a symphony–complete harmony. It was as if Thommy and Amalie connected "Brad Pitt" and "Barcelona" when they touched their fingers together at the center of the stage.

The hosts then asked "Brad Pitt" to listen to "Barcelona's" thoughts. "Barcelona" picked a card out of a box. He said nothing, keeping the contents of the card to himself. On the other side of the stage, "Brad Pitt" was asked what "Barcelona's" card said. She looked nervous, afraid to get the wrong answer. She shrugged, "hair?" Finally, the big reveal. "Barcelona" announced his card: "hairspray."

Every moment between these two strangers established a connection, allowing them to communicate by transferring energy to each other. Recall Jung's collective unconscious. Our physical bodies do not remove us from sharing consciousness streams supported by thought, emotion, intent, memories, community, or world events of great magnitude. These two strangers created a link through which they were able to have the thoughts of one actualized in the other, communicating in that shared language.

Whereas the connection between "Brad Pitt" and "Barcelona" formed while they were sharing a space, the stage at a conference they were attending, connections between strangers can be triggered by all different types of events. A form of telepathy occurs during a mass reaction to an important event–think "collective grief" in response to a national tragedy–where the same thought is instilled in a mass of people at once, consciousnesses overlapping due to shared experience.

Cutting Through the Noise: Mediumship

One form telepathy takes is a variation of the type that plays out between people with close bonds. Such telepathy requires an acknowledgement of an important tenet: consciousness does not cease when the body no longer functions. Consciousness survives beyond the physical form. Although we do not know the exact mechanism of how consciousness travels after leaving the body, we know that it reunites with the mass consciousness, becoming part of the material in the collective unconscious.

This is why so many religions are the same–they are all slightly different interpretations of that which exists in the collective unconsciousness. The difference in religions is the same as the difference in "Old Wise Man" archetypes: it's minimal. Still, the fundamental truth remains that our physical life is just a period when our consciousness is divided between the physical realm and the mass consciousness; eventually, we just return to the mass consciousness. Religions take this concept of the mass unconscious, sometimes perverting it to stoke fear and command conformity, and they dress it up, but it still produces the same construct of the afterlife.

I know this is not an easy concept to grasp.

Religion works to create a binary wherein there is a "right" way to perceive the afterlife, and all of life is a task in optimizing afterlife outcomes. Through their monopoly of the afterlife, they extend their dominion over what is "right" in how to think and live. This is why so many religions fear psi ability–for if we can communicate and connect with the consciousness of those whose bodies no longer work, then we can discover the truth for ourselves. If each of our consciousnesses becomes part of the mass consciousness, and the mass consciousness is ever-changing, then we can change after our physical demise. Then, there is no incentive to follow a specific religion's teaching because everyone reaches the same place after they leave their physical body. Hierarchies are dissolved. The afterlife is democratized. We are bestowed the gift of choice.

When I have a client seeking mediumship through spirit communication, sometimes the spirits have already tuned in telepathically and are waiting for me to open up the lines of communication to their loved ones.

However, when a client wants to connect with a specific individual, having a photo of that person can enhance my ability to establish a link. The picture is like Find-My-iPhone–it can't show you the exact location, but it can give you the general area. Then, I tap into the energy given to me by the client about their target, slinging it at the area conjured by the picture. The client's energy relays thoughts, feelings, and a sense of personality about their target that formulates the final filter to facilitate accurate spirit communication.

A silent phone is the rarer case. Often, numerous voices emerge, peppering the space with their instruments. When multiple spirits are using similar instruments, the tunes can get muddled. A couple of weeks before writing this chapter, I had such an experience. When the client joined the meeting, I immediately felt the presence of two spirits. I thought I was communicating with one: her name sounded like "Betty." She was the client's grandma and passed away from a health issue affecting her kidney. So, I started telling this client about all the information I was getting from this conscious energy pattern. The client looked at me with a furrowed brow of recognition.

From her reactions, I realized what was happening. I didn't have two polite people waiting to take turns to communicate. I was listening to two instruments trumpeting at the same time, so similar they sounded almost the same. Yes, the client did have a grandma named Betty, but she also had a grandma named Betsy. They both passed from similar ailments, and they had many life experiences in common, including marrying into the other's family. Their harmony in life became harmony in death.

Spirit communication is often made to be much more complicated than it is–but it is just telepathy that needs a connection with a higher state of consciousness than human or animal telepathy. Imagine how many candles are wasted each year for seances. Of course, it is important to find the environment that allows you to reach the psychic state needed to be open to spiritual telepathy. But that certainly does not *require* six $30 cucumber mint Yankee Candles or one ordained by a high priestess…*unless* the scent of those candles is part of your ritual for getting into the right psychic state.

CHAPTER 6

The Psychic Mind & Deciphering Its Symbol Code

Enabling Notifications on the Psychic Mind App

Our minds are like smartphones. Without anything downloaded onto them, they still have some basic features. Over time, more applications are added. Eventually, some get deleted to save space. We turn off notifications for other apps but allow some notifications to reach us even in our deepest concentration modes. Memories are stored. Messages come in. Favorite contacts change. We're always connected to the Cloud, to the internet, or to our cellular networks, enabling a near-constant exchange of data and information with the world around us and within ourselves.

At the end of the day, our minds, like our phones, are engaging in a constant struggle to deliver what is most relevant to our present situation. In the wild, it was the task of giving us the information that would maximize our chances of survival—we focused on the most important task of staying alive before moving on to secondary tasks. Now, our "survival" is mostly automatic. We work, get money, buy food, pay rent, and sleep cyclically. Once those are taken care of, we think about what we're going to read or watch on TV, what concert we're attending next, or that weird look some guy in a red fedora gave us on the subway...we've filled up the space we used to save for our instincts with things that are not *necessary*. We are crowding ourselves so much with constant avenues for external stimulation that we barely have time to listen to ourselves think.

Our psychic ability is like an app native to our phone, just like Alarm or Calculator. In your mind's thought and energy exchange, the Psychic Mind is constantly sending and receiving information. The first problem is, as we've discussed, that we've been told from a young age that psychic abilities are silly or useless, so we turn the notifications off and remove the app from our Home screen, hiding it deep in a folder on the third page.

Then, we have another layer of issues stemming from the long-term habit of ignoring or suppressing psychic communications–they've been coming in, but we have been so conditioned to ignore them that they just become background noise–so notifications are muted. We may get a notification that our UberEats order is downstairs on "Do Not Disturb," but we haven't opened "My Psychic Mind" in decades, even though we had that buzzy feeling a few weeks ago when our partner brought us home Flaming Hot Cool Ranch Doritos. (I swear they're not sponsoring me, but if they're reading this…I'm available!) We write it off–a ghost vibration, if you will.

So how do we tune back in to our psychic minds? How do we re-enable notifications to receive psychic information, tapping into the streams of thought that give us intuitive insight, psychic information, and spirit contact?

It's All About Intention

Maybe the chapter subheading spoiled it, but the answer is– INTENTION. We are *constantly* receiving and sending psychic information. This information can come when we tune into it, and it can come while we're sleeping. Maybe we're halfway through a marathon. Maybe we're on the couch, eating…Doritos. Psi ability is just a sense. We touch things every day, but we don't always pay attention to the feeling of what we touch. The doorknob is cold and hard. The lotion is thick and goopy. The orange is dimply and a little squishy. Our attention is diverted–we're focused on turning the doorknob, applying the lotion, on peeling the orange, or maybe on the new Beyonce track in the background (she still hasn't released the visuals)–not on the tactile sensations involved in the process. Accessing your psi ability is about focusing your mind–it's about putting in the active effort to notice all that is around you. Mindfulness, not mindlessness.

In the beginning, tuning into the Psychic Mind will result in a flood of notifications. There will be a continuous stream of incoming information. Some of the information will be meant for you and relevant to you personally. Other information will feel different, sitting inconsistently with your usual thought patterns and cycles. All of this psychic information will bombard you at once, like an unending social media feed, demanding attention from all of your senses. It can be *overwhelming*.

Since we cannot possibly dig through all of this psychic information at once, we must choose to "tune in" to a single event using our psychic mind, keeping the frame of reference limited and allowing for irrelevant information to fall away. Just like with regular sensing where we cannot record every detail of every experience but, rather, record "highlights" of a given memory, we cannot comprehend the complete picture formed by all the psychic information received at a given moment. We can process and must focus on processing only that which lies within our psychic focal range, directing our energy toward what we can capture instead of lamenting all that has escaped.

Setting the right intention helps anchor our practice, telling us what to focus on. Meditation helps the psychic mind decipher what information is meant for you as you navigate the flow of thoughts. Meditation is the reminder of your intention, and vice versa, making space for awareness of information outside your daily thought patterns. Thus, we've maximized the probability of receiving relevant psychic information and our ability to retain it.

Awareness Through Active Meditation Practices

If you're the type of person I think would be most likely to pick up this book, you've meditated before. You've sat in silence, focused on your breath, closed your eyes, sank into an easy posture, and tried to think about nothing. But this is only one form of meditation.

In the book "Spirited," Psychic Medium Rebecca Rosen delves into a practice I refer to as "active meditation." Active meditation is about concentration, not reacting to all the bullshit going on around us. It is the process of letting our mind be aware of the thoughts in front of it, aware of what is happening, ceasing judgment of those ideas, and following them wherever they go. Active meditation can occur when the body is doing something but the mind is not. By incorporating movement, active meditation helps quiet the mind and cultivate awareness. For example, you can engage in active meditation while doing an activity like dishwashing or running. All that matters is that the movement of the body is not taking up too much of the mind's energy.

Active meditation can take a variety of forms. It may involve intentional movement, like yoga or tai chi, where the focus is more on channeling the physical energy to release tension and promote relaxation. It may involve unintentional movement–movement not following a predetermined form–like automatic writing, drawing, or freeform dancing. For many, the balance between mind and body promotes unity, connection, and transcendence. Regardless of the method, the result is the reduction of mental clutter and stress.

Rosen discusses how, through automatic writing, she can distinguish between the voice of her personality (the "ego self") and the voice of a spirit (the "disembodied extra-ego consciousness"). Automatic writing is her chosen form of active meditation. Although the term sounds fancy and inaccessible, automatic writing just involves scribbling, to engage in the anxious parts of yourself. This process allows your focus and energy to shift, directing your attention to what is happening inside your brain. Sometimes the writing reflects whatever dialogue is happening inside of the mind. Other times, it just looks like scribbles. Whatever feels right at that moment *is* right.

Automatic writing induces a trance state. The induced trance state occurs when the brain is fixated on a specific train of thought while engaged in active meditation. Instead of normal meditation, which can involve awareness of surface-level thoughts, a trance state requires digging beneath those thoughts to the ideas floating beneath the surface. This will sound like engaging in an inner dialogue, hyperfixating on the thought pattern, and tunneling through it.

Automatic writing naturally slows our attention down. We fixate on transposing what is flowing through our minds, taking the nebulous and putting it into a concrete, written form. By doing this, we also become even more aware of our thought stream. Then, over time, we're able to notice the subtle changes that occur in real time within our thought streams. Soon, we can begin to detect what is our "voice" or thought pattern versus what is a foreign thought pattern.

Recognizing Our Own Voice(s)

Okay, I know I just threw *another* new term at you. In my defense, this book is about learning! So, what's a thought pattern? And what's a thought stream? Are they the same?

Great questions!

A thought stream is exactly what it sounds like: a river flowing constantly of our thoughts, messy, chaotic, and unorganized.

A thought pattern is sticking a bucket into that stream and examining what's in that bucket. A thought pattern is a series of thoughts that, when viewed alone, begin to form a coherent thought, structure, or idea. Multiple thought patterns may link to each other, though, even if they seem unrelated.

The concept of a thought pattern is easiest for me to explain because I have ADHD. Imagine this: I'm making eggs. I get what I need to make the eggs. That's a thought pattern.

Egg.
Pan.
Pan needs heat.
Need to turn over egg.
Must leave egg in pan for specific time.
Egg will be done.

Need plate.
Plate to hold egg after pan.

Great. As I'm cooking the egg, I start to think, how did they make the canola oil into a spray that has no calories? I wish I knew how to crack an egg with one hand–it looks so cool. Smoke is rising from the pan. Is it going to set off the smoke alarm? Is there a way for a smoke alarm to know when it is normal cooking smoke versus dangerous fire smoke? Look at the tree outside the window! It looks like it needs a trim. Trimming requires scissors. But, like big scissors. When was the last time I cut my hair? I definitely need to clean up my fade. I wonder if Patty is available for a touch-up. Verizon is just the worst in Santa Fe lately. Remember when there were more phone companies? Time to flip over this egg. I never feel like I get this part right because I break the yolk around 30% of the time. It's a real gamble. I need a back massage.

My thoughts may branch out–like from the act of cracking an egg to watching the smoke from the egg rise, following the natural conclusion of rising smoke in an enclosed space. I can follow those thoughts down that thought pattern. I could get interrupted by a new thought pattern–tree trimming to calling Patty for a touch-up for my fade–and follow that for a spell. And the thoughts may return to the original pattern, as I flip over the egg, my attention refocuses. Even if we do not stay on the branched-out thought patterns, we are aware that they may mean something ("I need a haircut") or nothing ("cracking an egg with one hand looks cool").

With enough practice becoming aware of our thoughts through active meditation, we're able to focus on even the tiniest changes in our thought stream–the true blips of information that dance for a millisecond across our consciousness. We become truly aware of what's related to our actions and how our behaviors feed into one another. Our self-awareness begets mental sensitivity.

In psychic sensing, we may be in a place where we're following a thought pattern when another one appears that does not seem to fit. What do we do with that information? Well, it may not fit, but our sense is picking up on *something*, and while it may not be the thing to focus on at that moment, it may be something worth returning to. As we develop our psi abilities, we can pay attention to those blips, return to them, and follow them in whatever direction they go. I practice this process enough that when I intend to sense psychically, my brain switches modes by default. I hyper-fixate on those blips, which I've come to identify as my psychic "sweet spot."

What's Your Motivation?

In understanding the processes of your own mind, it is essential to uncover the "why" behind your thoughts and actions. Meditation will help you distill the "sponsoring motivation"–the lens through which you see the world that pushes you to act. Once we identify our sponsoring motivations, we can work to isolate them and untangle them from interfering with our psychic senses.

Perhaps one of these is your sponsoring motivation:

- **Fear or worry:** You act out of a need to avoid an outcome or obstacle.
- **Desire or pleasure:** You act to achieve a certain physical sensation.
- **Greed:** You act to preserve yourself, to make sure you are satisfied.
- **Curiosity:** You act to know or investigate the world, seeking to understand.
- **Acceptance:** You act to achieve the approval of others.
- **Insecurity:** You act to externalize your internal distortions.
- **Recognition/Pride:** You act to inflate your social status because you desire acknowledgement.

There are more sponsoring motivations, and many may be acting together at one moment. A sponsoring motivation of acceptance can make you more susceptible to the influence of others. Conversely, a sponsoring motivation of fear/worry may be accompanied by the need for acceptance that created the fear.

For example, you might want a partner. So, you start dating for this purpose. You are dating because you are afraid of being alone. You want to fit into our society that is built around monogamous partnerships. You worry that not finding a partner indicates a fundamental unsuitability for love. A comment, look, or touch from your date can unleash a torrent of thoughts and their related thought patterns in our minds. Suddenly, your mind went from hearing, "Why are you still single?" to seeing yourself in a cold, dark room, a tear falling down your wrinkly cheek as you lay dying alone.

Not being able to understand and untangle your sponsoring motivation can lead to inaccurate sensing. I once knew someone who, in my opinion, was motivated by recognition. They wanted people to know their name and to associate them with greatness. They moved like the breeze envied their coolness. With such a defined belief in themselves, they never operated as if they could be incorrect. Their readings were chances to get attention for themselves, not to help others. Unsurprisingly, this led to reading where the details they sensed were accurate but the narrative spun from those details was inaccurate. They made a big prediction to gain attention, claiming someone had been raped, without taking the time to understand what the information they were sensing truly meant, clouded by their desire for a dramatic conclusion. The truth was that the person simply had consensual sex with their boyfriend. Not the trauma of rape. It ultimately led to this psychic dropping out of a developmental class that would have benefitted them greatly, too concerned with salvaging their pride than the growing pains accompanying psychic potential.

Ego is fine in moderation. With a sponsoring motivation like Recognition/Pride, it can become so repetitive as to bury itself within us. Eventually, we become unable to detect it as it merges into part of our personality–part of our sense of self. But, through meditation comes a level of self-awareness through increasing mental sensitivity. You become able to recognize the differences in your thought patterns and are able to trace their source and motivation. Once you can identify what comes from within you, it is easier to identify that which comes from outside. Psychic information, as derived from our extrasensory senses, may emerge in our thought stream in conflict with our usual motivational drives or in dissonance with our previous thought patterns. Heightened conscious awareness through meditation facilitates detection, changing the way we react to the world around us and tuning ourselves to the subtle influences of our psychic senses.

If we are not attuned to what is our "normal" thought processes, we will miss the psychic influences lying outside of our normal thought stream.

No one starts with the ability to fully receive and comprehend every psychic signal received from every psychic sense. Practice is vital to transform from indecipherable blobs of data to accurate psychic sensing. Only from consistent practice can we learn how to accurately lock into the correct frequency and increase the speed of translating psychic information.

Advanced Exercises: Remote Viewing

"Practice, Practice, Practice." But how should we practice? Just like a sport, we exercise our psychic muscles. Clairvoyance, telepathy, precognition. Early in my psychic career, I made the fantastic decision to train under the mentorship of a far more seasoned psychic, Pam Coronado. Young and ambitious, studying under a mentor enriched my developing practice with vital insight and, crucially, *focus*. Pam taught me so many things and enabled me to be the psychic I am today, but the most valuable gift I received from her was the practice of Remote Viewing.

Remote viewing is "target sensing." The term specifically refers to the protocol developed by the Stanford Research Institute (SRI). The Department of Defense started funding experiments at the Stanford Research Institute in 1978, culminating in what would eventually be called the CIA's Operation Stargate.[16] Operation Stargate aimed to leverage remote viewing for "intelligence"

---

[16] There was also Project Grill Flame, a Defense Intelligence Agency effort investigating psychoenergetics phenomenon. It is considered within the Stargate umbrella. https://www.cia.gov/readingroom/docs/CIA-RDP96-00788R001100510002-3.pdf

purposes during the Cold War. Pam is a disciple of this school of remote sensing, and some of her mentors were on the US's team of Psychic Spies involved in Operation Stargate.

The CIA's interest in remote viewing started with Robert Monroe. Monroe, a radio operator, started exploring altered states of consciousness. In his growing fascination with out-of-body experiences, he developed a method called Hemi-Sync (short for Hemispheric Synchronization). Hemi-Sync uses audio frequencies to synchronize the brain's hemispheres; it's complicated, but the idea is that the brain operates at different frequencies based on its state of activity, so sounds of different frequencies ("auditory stimulation") may alter the brain's frequency to promote altered states of consciousness.

Monroe's Hemi-Sync methodology was used in Operation Stargate[17] as a gateway experience, triggering a state of consciousness within the body that allows the mind to leave the physical body to travel to a different point in time and space. Operation Stargate was helmed by Ingo Swann, Russell Targ, and Harold Puthoff. While Swann was an artist and psychic, Targ and Puthoff came from traditional physics backgrounds. Together, they developed a protocol for remote viewing, centering on the "coordinate method" to describe a remote location. The evidence gleaned from these studies was used by the government, likely to take satellite photographs of the coordinates of enemy locations, though the full extent of this use remains unclear.

Controlled remote viewing is a common variation of remote reviewing based on Swann's techniques. This method occurs in multiple stages. The first stage is "tasking": the target of the session is defined and described to establish the focus. The second step is "reception": the individual enters into a state of deep relaxation, perhaps by using sensory deprivation or meditation to reach this

---

[17] "STAR GATE PROJECT: AN OVERVIEW" (30 Apr 1993). https://www.cia.gov/readingroom/docs/CIA-RDP96-00789R002800180001-2.pdf

state. The individual then will write down their impressions, details, feelings, or imagery. The third step is "collection": the information gained on the target is gathered, analyzed, and reflected upon.

Pam is part of an International Remote Viewing Association, so the method of remote viewing she taught me is a mix of that used by the Psychic Spies in Project Stargate and that of the organization. Because the goal of her viewing is missing people or bodies, not military targets, her approach differs from the "coordinate" method in Stargate. Instead, she focuses on the target (the missing person or crime) and then looks to find the target in the past, facilitating her description of the surrounding circumstances and environment of the crime.

Pam taught us to fixate on details that our minds gathered in response to the target. Pam wasn't concerned with the story we sensed–she cared only about how the details we sensed connected to the target. Whereas Psychic spies were given numbers to determine what the target was, Pam would give us the number assigned to a missing person's case and ask us to get the details about the target/missing person. Each week she would assign new target exercises, and we would respond with details we had sensed. We broke each exercise into basic elements such as shapes, colors, textures, feelings, and so on. Once we sensed enough usable information, Pam would reveal the answer to gauge our progress. Occasionally, people dropped out when they weren't immediately successful, but, for me, repeating these exercises was key to unlocking my full psychic potential.

Today, I don't find myself looking for bodies very often. When I engage in remote viewing, I tune into the events of a person's life, sense their experience within that moment, feel their emotions, think their thoughts, and attempt to grasp the who-what-where-when-why of that individual's current place in life. As if I were "consciousness swapping," I'm able to experience things from their perspective. Through this, I can check in with their future lives, emphasizing experiences, and bringing balance to their emotionally-charged perspectives. I'm not like a Psychic Spy looking for every literal component of the scenario so we don't bomb the wrong place. I'm searching for the heart of the matter.

On a recent Instagram Live reading, a woman came on to ask about her grandchild: he was having a terrible pain in his stomach and had missed the past two weeks of school. As the question came to me, I used remote viewing to see myself inside the child's body, looking around. I tried to find something that seemed extraordinary and kept searching until I felt something that *wasn't* his physical self. Suddenly, I saw my memories of being molested as a child. Immediately following that, I got a memory of being bullied and a different memory of an experience as an adult getting an STI. We talked later that night, and I told her that I believed he was being bullied at school. Perhaps by someone being sexually inappropriate with him, touching him in a way he doesn't like. The woman had a feeling he was being bullied, and she'd already had a conversation with him where he'd confessed a person on the bus was being inappropriate with him. But, after speaking with me, she knew that she needed to sit down with him to get to the root of his tummy issues.

The most important thing to remember with remote viewing is that it gets easier over time as you develop your skills and learn to trust yourself. Often, we want to know everything right away. That clouds our ability to psychic sense. Some things, however, take time to reveal themselves. While we may want to jump to conclusions about a story, the best way to remote view is to look at all of the details you receive, study them, and then make your best educated guess based on those details.

We are used to living every moment of our lives perceiving situations and experiences. Psychic sensing, through Pam's method, requires us to focus on the elements and details and then make an educated guess based on those details and not on our "story." Set your intention, don't fear being less than 100% accurate, and the details will come.

The Mind Space Psychic Sensing Exercise

When studying under Pam in the early stages of my professional practice, there was this one exercise that pushed me to a new level. At first, I completely bombed. We were supposed to be making attempts at sensing details, but I'd get lost in my mental madness. Instead of arriving at the intended location, I'd be ten miles away, off the shore, longing for the day when I'd sense the "right" things.

To expand our capacity to psychically sense, we must hone our ability to engage in active awareness and meditation. While Pam's version of this exercise centered on "Phase I," I've modified the exercise to include two additional phases, "Phase II" and "Phase III." I've experienced great growth from my three-phase method. Professionally, I've witnessed it positively impact my students, especially by helping those new to sensing overcome their blocks with greater ease.

Before I go any deeper, know that you may suck at first, just like I did. The answer to this exercise is at the end of this chapter. But, you only do yourself a disservice by seeking the answer first. This exercise is not about getting the answer. This exercise is about mastering the practice—about learning how your abilities work, activating them quickly, and understanding them accurately.

Now, grab a pencil (or pen) and paper. We're going to be stepping out of our active meditation state several times to note our observations. My words in these pages will be guiding you the entire time, too. Just remember to write down *whatever* comes up for you along the way, even (*and especially*) if it seems insignificant.

We will be going to a place called the "Mind Space." In Phase I, we'll examine our "target" in our Mind Space. In Phases II and III, we'll bring our own memories into the mind space for examination. Our goal is to uncover our mental madness (i.e., the unconscious and often symbol-heavy language our mind uses to communicate with us), so we can glean greater meaning from what appears in our Mind Space.

To settle into our Mind Space, we must first find a relaxed state. We need to enter active meditation, so do whatever you need to be comfortable. Stretch out, recline, or whatever else feels good to you. It's not something to overthink. If closing your eyes feels right, then do that, but you do not need to. I will often fixate on a point outside the window, my focus blurring at the point where the bright, seemingly endless blue sky meets the green, mountainous peaks of New Mexico's natural splendor. Staring at a point on the wall will work too. Keep your mind firm but soft: activate the part of it that you use when imagining or visualizing your future.

Even if your eyes are open, imagine that what you're seeing is a completely dark room inside of your mind. No light. No identifiable structures. No windows. No mountains. Just black. If this image isn't coming to you, think of a time you walked into a place and thought, "Shit, it's dark in here. I need to find the light switch." That's where you are. That room. That dark, dimensionless room is the Mind Space.

Phase I

Be in the Mind Space. Take one last second to absorb its darkness before lifting your arm to your right. You feel the light switch, changing it to the "ON" position with a soft application of pressure. A spotlight cascades in from above, piercing the center of the room. Pure darkness shrouds everything untouched by the concentrated beam of light. Despite the luminescence, there are still no walls, no depth, and no corners. Only a single, solitary source of light.

Beneath your spotlight is your "target." The "target" is a number sequence. These numbers represent *something*, and your task will be to sense details of that something from the target. The target—the number sequence—is the only thing that you see in the spotlight.

For this exercise, your target is 281.

Write this number sequence down on your paper to help you focus, set your intention, and begin to connect this target with associated information.

Now tune in to the target: 281. Write down anything and everything that comes to you.

Ask yourself questions. "What do you represent, 281?" "What are your connections, 281?" Write down anything that occurs in response to these questions.

If nothing happens, that's fine! Just let your mind wander, pay attention to your thoughts, and note what comes to you.

Are you thinking of an idea? Are you thinking of a shape? Are you thinking of a color? Are you thinking of a memory triggered by the number? Are your thoughts still focused on the earlier events of your day? Are you distracted by what was happening right before you began the exercise? Are you already certain you know what this image is, and you've concluded that you have the correct answer?

Your job is to observe without judgment, probe, and document. DO NOT DISMISS ANYTHING! Even if you think something is completely strange or irrelevant, write it down. Even if something is scary, uncomfortable, or emotionally painful, write it down. *Whatever* your mind brings to you, write it down.

Within these first moments of psychic sensing, you can be flooded with emotions unrelated to what you're trying to sense involving present problems, past trauma, and anxieties about the future. These emotions underlie energy patterns occupying space in our subconscious, and they often mix with information from our psychic senses. Eliminate self-induced blocks by giving yourself time to process your emotions, unclouding your psychic senses and refocusing your intention on your target.

Phase II

Phase I will become easier with practice; it is difficult to train the mind to procure details with only an intention set. In the beginning of your psychic journey, you are still working with intuition as your primary tool for psychic sensing. It will take many mental muscle repetitions to skillfully bypass any self-induced blocks. In the meantime, Phases II and III will help jumpstart your mind muscles into sensing mode.

Spend some time looking through the initial impressions you've written down so far. Reflect for a moment.

Now, return to your Mind Space. A blank TV sits in the center of the room, powered off with nothing on the screen. Turn it on. Witness the brightness increase in intensity, spreading to each corner. You recognize what's playing on the screen.

Stop. What do you see on the screen?

Let your memory bring you something familiar from your past—a memory of a show or movie you've seen before—and hold this moment in your mind. Focus on each precise moment of the scene now playing in your mind.

As you analyze the moment of the movie selected by your mind and placed on your Mind Space's TV, focus on what the elements of the scene represent. Ask yourself: What are the highlights of the scene? What are some of the details that stand out to you? Is it the activity of a character? Is there an object that draws your attention? Is there a memorable color? Outfit? A prevailing mood? Try to analyze without relation to storyline, plot, or character; the relevant context is limited to what is played on the screen.

Write down everything pulling your focus in vivid detail.

Phase III

Each Phase may produce distinctive results; so, do not discard something because it feels disconnected from what you've already sensed. Sensing is about details, not about instantaneously absorbing a fully formed image. Completing our Phase I Initial Perceptions and Phase II Media Memories, our written observations may seem disjointed, but we must release our desire for conclusion.

Drift into your Mind Space clear from the remnants of ideas, themes, and elements unearthed in Phases I and II. Relax. Recall the target. 281. Relax. It floats alone.

Now, let your mind wander until it brings back a moment from your life. Whatever moment it presents is right. Don't judge the moment. Hold the moment. Put it on the TV from Phase II. Play it. Play it again. Again.

Recall the contours of the memory and write them down as they bubble up.

If you need help with grabbing details, ask yourself what type of memory you're reviewing. Is it a past experience? Is it focusing on a place? Is it focusing on a person? Where were you? What were you doing? What were you experiencing? What is before you? What are the highlights of this moment in your past? Again, forget the storyline or where this event occurred in the timeline of your life. Recall only the elements of the moment. Does anything command your focus? A color, shape, object, motion, mood, or feeling?

Your mind chose this moment for a reason. Your mind is communicating to you through this choice. Focus on where your mind is fixating and write it down.

Sensory Review

Congratulations on completing Phases I, II, and III.

I hope you enjoy your new real estate—a Mind Space is incredibly valuable territory. It is a unique environment where your mind can communicate with you using its own language, a language formulated by unique symbols birthed from your life's experiences, mental associations, and the collective unconscious. You may arrive at the same conclusion as someone else despite your Mind Spaces showing completely different symbols. Your mind is your three-dimensional experience; your interpretation gives it meaning. That's why there is no reason to dismiss what you've received—even if it's not 100% accurate, your mind is still providing you with more information about how to decode its symbols.

Spending time practicing exercises like this in your Mind Space will help you harness your mind's raw power to unlock powerful psychic abilities.

Turn to your notes. Take some time to look them over. Write down what you think your mind was trying to communicate through the details you wrote down. Examine their patterns and peculiarities for common threads, harmonies, and discords. Does this give any insight into what 281 might be?

SPOILER ALERT!

(Do not proceed to the next page until you've completed the exercise.)

Target 281

If at First You Don't Succeed...Try Again

The bird is the physical image of what your mind was attempting to sense psychically through the "target," 281.

If you got it, wonderful! If you didn't, wonderful! As I said before, I was awful when I first started exercises like this. Being so bad had the consequence of making me strive to be better.

Continue this exercise independently by collecting images of simple objects to start. Then, you can move to the scenes with events or people engaging in activities. Have a friend assign you random numbers to the images and do the exercise as I've outlined here. Again, I repeat, you *will* get better through practice. You will become faster. Your details will become more direct. Your abilities will continue to develop.

In doing this exercise alone, you'll notice changes in your daily life: you'll have more moments of psychic insight from random everyday experiences, become more intuitive, and experience more psychic occurrences. It's much easier to run up a hill on a casual walk when you've put in hours on a Stairmaster. Like a full-body gym workout, this is a full psychic ability exercise: your entire psychic self will be strengthened through practice and better able to use the tools available to it. Regardless of how the exercise turned out for you, you must give yourself grace and flexibility and applaud yourself for pushing yourself into something new.

Psychic Sensing & The Myth Around "Blockages"

I previously mentioned how we often remain in the comfort of our reality bubbles and must work to pop them to trigger psychic phenomena. Experiences of trauma, shock, surprise, novelty, or deep vulnerability may result in this bubble-pop. For some, the popped reality bubble may be a slow leak, gradually opening them up to experiences that transcend societal conformity.

What pops the reality bubble is called a trigger. Once the bubble pops, a trigger operates to continue to open the mind. From a trigger comes all psychic sensing.

The trigger is the invisible hand that turns on the faucet. It begins the process of sensing. It may be spontaneous or conjured, but it must occur for the sensing to flow. Our internal response to the trigger is a form of energy intention. When confronted with a trigger, our intention may take two routes: (1) to seek to understand through obtaining knowledge and maintaining awareness, or (2) to attempt to limit the effect of the trigger and try to minimize its overwhelming circumstances. Fight or flight.

Just like "fight or flight," our responses to triggers are ingrained in ourselves and conditioned by our experiences, meaning that when we gain new experiences ("coping mechanisms" or other tools that help guide the mind toward productive ends), we can change the way the trigger affects our perception.

Sudden experiences of psychic insight may *feel* mysterious and random, but they stem from the same processes of the mind we've already discussed. Something is *activating* sensing through a trigger, an almost automatic response; the hard part is keeping the mind *open* throughout the sensing process.

Pringles was wrong. Once you pop, the fun *can* stop. Maybe that's why I prefer Doritos...

Just Believe and Go Get Your Money Back

Lay off the Pringles. Lay off the crystals, candles, cards, and ceremonies. Lay off the idea of a perfect ritual or a perfect vision. Now, let me save you some time and money.

Simple *intention* is the key to activating psychic ability. The intention to be open, to communicate, and to go where led. Choosing to be curious about a thing allows the mind to begin to know a thing.

You are not blocked because you have not been initiated into the mystical order of the oracle at Delphi. You are not blocked because you are somehow unworthy. You are not blocked because you lack ability. The people that try to sell you a ceremony in Sedona, surprise(!), don't have a monopoly on psychic ability. They do, however, have a monetary incentive to make you think that you're nothing without them, and they'll take your money despite knowing that is not true.

Let's all say it together: EVERYONE has the ABILITY to be PSYCHIC. That's the thesis of this book. It's already in you. If you're able to think, you're able to sense. So, I guess not *everyone* can be psychic, but you get the picture.

If you believe that you cannot do something, the mind will activate and follow your lead. And learning with the right tools gives the mind the right access to hone its innate skills. For learning to be effective, belief must be there first and foremost.

SUCCESS = BELIEF + PRACTICE

Now, go get your refund for that overpriced geode. I know it's very sparkly, but it's not getting you closer to psychic sensing.

Slaying Demons to Battle the Blockage

If you struggle to release your control over the psychic process because you're afraid something terrible will happen, you'll block your abilities. If you were raised in a very superstitious or religious environment where you were told psychic activities were evil and have not confronted and corrected that teaching, you'll block your abilities. If you believe you are not special enough to be psychic, you'll block your abilities. If you want to avoid being wrong, you'll block your abilities. If you expect that you'll be as good as the psychics and mediums on TV despite being fresh out of the gate, you'll block your abilities.

Are we feeling confident? Good. Confidence is necessary to overcome the dreaded blockage because, in many ways, overcoming a blockage requires battling long-held demons by understanding and discrediting their origins. It's not an easy process, but it will leave you feeling healthier, happier, and able to take your abilities to the next level.

Blockages can be dense and layered, like an onion. The outermost blockages are those formed by societal influences. Think of these as the thinnest barriers–customs, laws, societal structures, norms, and other things that push us to conform. For example, we live in a heteronormative society in the United States that is structured around the idea of a male-female pairing that marries, produces children, consumes goods, pays taxes, and dies, with their children taking their place, entering into a male-female marriage, producing children, consuming goods, paying taxes, and the cycle continues. It is this structure that ensures schools are funded, but it also makes it difficult for non-mainstream ideas to thrive. What "has been" works, so we shouldn't mess with the formula.

Now, imagine being queer and experiencing attraction outside of the male-female dichotomy. The existing structures in the United States are not made for you to thrive. We are told in our schools that gay people have sex that doesn't lead to children, that sex will lead to HIV, and HIV is a death sentence; we do not educate on the advances in medication or the effectiveness of Truvada/PREP. If we have gay sex, we can't have children! And if we die, we can't pay taxes!

The fear of transgressing the societal norm of heterosexuality is a blockage. Luckily, it can be overcome through therapy and RuPaul's Drag Race.

As you probably realize, for most people, a single blockage may penetrate many layers. The second type of blockage exists in a deeper layer of self. This is a communal blockage. These barriers are formed by concepts that exist closer to the center of the self, like lessons taught by parents or religion, the traditions of your geographic area, or the norms of your community. Think of them as societal blockages on a more intimate level, making them harder to overcome.

Imagine being queer again. It's not just that society is built around heterosexual partnerships that causes a blockage between the person and their fullest expression. Maybe growing up in a religious community that condemned homosexuality as the devil's work was an influence. Add the impact of growing up around other kids who believed and repeated those same lessons at school and in the streets. Then, consider the pressure of a mom who expects you will have (heterosexual) sex, make children, and pay taxes!

The blockage, in a way, was formed as a maladaptive protection. It protects the self from fully realizing that their desire or identity is incompatible with the values thrust upon them. With any protective coating, breaking the blockage risks exposure to new elements. While initially a frightening proposition, it is exactly that exposure that facilitates psychic sensing.

The last type of blockage is a blockage created by the self. This self-block is the worst cockblock you can have. Simply, this is you doubting yourself. It could be a function of past trauma or a negative mindset that won't allow you to believe in yourself. It could be a deep fear of your own success and what that will mean for you and the people around you. It could be insecurity, feeling as if you aren't qualified or "special" enough to tap into your psychic senses;

insecurity may also be doubting the accuracy of your readings, so afraid to say or do something wrong that you freeze yourself into doing nothing at all.

Again, imagine being queer. You have the blockages from society and community, but you also developed self-blockages. Part of the self-blockage came from a traumatic experience you had as a child where you were called names because you preferred to play with the girls. Part of the self-blockage comes from a fear that living your truth will not do anything to ease your unhappiness. Part of the self-blockage is your inability to imagine a future where you're able to be free and open–a fear of not knowing who you could become.

Sometimes, people will confuse a self-block for an external block. They'll say, "Oh, my family was cursed by a witch in the 1600s, so, until that curse is cleared up, I won't be able to sense." My dear friend, your block may be related to issues stemming from your family–maybe you feared disappointing your father and became a perfectionist as a result, steered by a fear of failing instead of by a desire to grow–but this block exists within you at the deepest level. It has penetrated your mind and, as a result, has impacted your sensing. It's easier to blame the circumstances than to look critically at the self.

In a way, every blockage becomes a self-block over time–the block becomes internalized. The longer it goes unaddressed, the more it causes you to turn part of yourself off, yet it is that part that you need to access: your deepest, most empathetic and vulnerable humanity. Your readings will never be perfect, but you can give your best to the people you serve.

When you have a rough read, it is essential to take the time you need to process. If you need to cry, cry. You and your practice will be better for it. The most important thing is to surrender to the depth of feeling you are experiencing, whether it be shame, rejection, failure, or any other lower-level feelings. Then, remind yourself that this is part of the process of growth, evolution, and resilience. It hurts to fall, but life is a trampoline, and you can bounce back. The more effort you invest, the higher you bounce. You *are* better than your worst experience, and you will continue to get better through your practice.

BLOCKAGE TYPE	MEANING/SYMPTOMS
Unrealistic Expectations	Your BS notions of what it means to be psychic, learned from TV or otherwise, aren't aligning with your psychic sensing, so you do not believe you are actually using psychic sensing. This is the "Sixth Sense Syndrome." Just because our experiences do not match up to the movies does not make them less legitimate.
Control Freak Syndrome	This is my big one. You try to control all the pieces of being psychic, dictating how and what energy you receive. You can't let yourself be moved by the universe or go with the flow, so your desire for control prevents you from being a conduit for the universe. There's no ToC on ESP.[18]
Dismissing Thoughts & Memory	You dismiss things that come up in stages of sensing, refuse to acknowledge them, and instead focus only on what you *think* you're supposed to be sensing. With practice, your brain will start to associate symbols with certain concepts as a shorthand during sensing; if you dismiss what your brain

---

[18] ToC means Terms or Conditions. It's that long thing you read before making a new account for a website. ESP means extrasensory perception. I thought it was cute.

	offers you, you'll never begin to build your vocabulary.
Fear (Faith & Beliefs)	You are in fear of your full psychic potential. Maybe you grew up religious with a belief that certain things have value or that psychic activities are evil, dark, or devil-related. You feel like you're doing something wrong by engaging with psychic sensing.
	Maybe you grew up in a family of skeptics and non-believers that made you think that believing in psychic ability is crazy. You fear that your growing interest is crazy or maybe that you're mentally ill.
	Regularly, bring yourself to a place of peace by reminding yourself that you are beautiful, you are worthy, and that you have this ability whether you use it often or not. Nothing is wrong with you. You're not possessed. Everything that you're doing is right if it comes from a good intention.
Vulnerable to Negativity	You are going to come by haters and skeptics. You let their ideas permeate your intention. Sometimes, the hater comes from inside you, and you let it stay.
	When you do a reading, you must be operating from a place of love, wellness, and openness. Keep your intention positive. You may still experience negative things during sensing or may need to deliver news that is negative; still, they will flow from your intention of positivity, and

	it won't be able to wrap around you in the same way it would if it came from an intention marked by negativity.
Limiting Beliefs	You learned how to read from a book or a course. You cannot bend your practice away from what this specific book or specific teacher told you. You reject energy that does not conform to their teachings. Letting it guide you does not need to be letting it dictate you.
Unworthiness	You feel like you need to receive some sort of approval from others in the field or from a divine source before you may practice. You need certification. You need credentials. You need courses. You have to be blessed by a Shaman and be a Reiki Master. Psssst. You're already psychic. You're already good enough. You need practice to get better. I can't tell you if you're psychic or not–only you can make you believe that.
Unprocessed Trauma	You've been through trauma. Because of that trauma, some things are painful for you. Some things color your ability to experience fully. You have trauma responses that you haven't dealt with. Your trauma is guiding your sensing, causing you to see things (and maybe even clients) in a certain way. Your trauma is interfering with your concentration, overshadowing the shit you want to sense. Trauma makes us more sensitive and can be useful in sensing. But the

	trauma cannot hold power over you. You are over your trauma once you can speak on the experience in a way that doesn't bring up emotion or linger with you afterward. Acknowledging a past pain separates from feeling a present pain.
Guilt	People in your life have told you that being a psychic isn't real, valuable, or a viable career. You know of so many scammers in the field. Even though your intentions are pure, you feel like you shouldn't be getting paid for your skills. You believe the skeptics and doubt yourself, you internalize their distaste for the profession and repurpose it as a reason why you shouldn't be doing this at all. This block is common when people make the move from doing readings for free to becoming a paid psychic.
	People who provide a service get paid. When people don't provide a service, they don't get paid. If you have people paying for a service that keep paying for a service, they're receiving a service and wish to keep receiving the service. The longer you practice professionally, the more experience you'll be able to identify to keep this block away.
Desperation	You're trying to connect to a loved one or spirit but cannot make it happen. You believe that a wildly thriving psychic business is the only way you'll be able to live the life you want. This work must be fruitful or else you're not

special. You need that absolute piece of proof that this is real.

You're not special, and chasing validation is not going to make you feel special. It's going to make you feel empty. You are a psychic, just like everybody else. You don't have control over other people's feelings. Being a psychic is not a magic path to riches. But you are you, and that makes you special. Put that special part of you into your practice. Let your good intentions guide you. That's your best shot. Push yourself. Be your biggest cheerleader. Let your ego get just big enough to allow you to bounce back quickly from your low points. Be realistic. Be patient. Focus on developing your ability fully.

Dealing with the Blockage

We've already discussed identifying the blockage. Breaking the blockage down is the process of dissecting it into parts–societal, communal, and self. Now, we eradicate it by chipping away at the distortions that compose its foundation.

If you're experiencing a blockage, first identify what that blockage is. After you're able to name it, break it down further. What is *really* at the root of the blockage? Is it a fear of rejection or embarrassment? Did you have a traumatic experience as a child where you felt responsible for something bad happening, leading to fear and lingering guilt? A feeling of insecurity because you're not getting every detail of every reading perfect or feeling like your interpretation is wrong? Write it down. Then write three things that show how that blockage root is incorrect. Think about what you've done right. Give yourself grace in mistakes–you're still learning and growing. Remember the "why" you want to do this work–the *real* why.

I've seen so many people–from novices and wannabe psychics to experts–blocked by their "why." You must have a purpose that is strong enough to compel you to break the blockage, even when you're at your weakest point. A blockage is a function of mindset, which means you must get your mind right before you can overcome it.

Why do you want to be a psychic? If your answer is "attention" or to be "discovered" so you can have a show on TV and be the next Theresa Caputo, I have to tell you a tough truth: you need to work through your shit before you will ever be able to access your psychic abilities. If you don't, you'll never be more than a charlatan, seeking gratification for yourself over helping others. Your desire for "attention" means you need to work through your shit. You probably need to get past a deeper blockage that is causing you to seek external validation. An untempered ego is a symptom of a blockage.

Now, I'm not ego-less. I'm writing this book because I believe I have valuable insights to share, drawing from my expertise and experiences that can benefit others. That, in itself, is an act of ego. But, to get here, I had to work through my superiority bullshit and the related inferiority bullshit that caused me to try to heal my abused inner child through fame, fortune, and attention.

It was in the process of working through my own blockages that I was able to rediscover my sense of purpose and be able to truly start my psychic journey.

Psychic work is a form of healing. It is not about you. It should be about putting in the practice to become the best tool possible to help others. To pursue this field professionally is to embrace a lifetime commitment to your development, revere the work, accept praise gracefully, let go of jealousy, fear, and competitiveness, and to strive to give to others.

To be a professional psychic is to serve. The sooner you adopt that mindset and remember that your task is to be the best vessel possible for that service, the sooner you will be able to harness your psychic abilities.

How I Beat My Blocks

If you're blocked, don't worry. Smile. You have already identified that you're blocked. Step one, complete. Progress logged. You're going through an experience shared with the most accomplished psychics in history.

I had a self-blockage that lasted for ten years—an entire decade, but not forever. It took a while, but I broke free, and I am grateful for all that I learned about myself and my practice during that time.

After my first psychic experience with the kitchen fire, I began my psychic awakening. Curiosity about what I'd experienced led me to my high school library. I consumed everything I could get my hands on related to psychic phenomena, the supernatural, and psychic abilities. That wasn't enough. I soon found myself venturing into the city library to find more. Famous psychics and mediums like Sylvia Browne, James Van Praagh, George Anderson, and John Edwards were hitting the TV circuit. I'd sit, mesmerized, glued to the screen, watching these professionals in their specials, giving readings with ease and bringing closure to their audience. I wanted to be able to do that, too, but, while showing the fruits of their abilities, they rarely provided insight into the process–only John Edward provided a glimpse into how a reading would trigger his memories. From my studies, I believed I needed to sit and meditate to become more spiritual, and then, I would be able to be receptive to psychic information. I also believed that I would just intuitively know how to be psychic, and the information would be correct. At least that's what the psychics, mediums, and their edited TV readings portrayed. I believed in myself, even if I didn't know how much I didn't know.

So, I kept working on it. I would bury myself in deep meditation for hours at a time in the hopes of honing my abilities. One day, I received a call from my good friend Lawrence. He asked me what I'd been doing, and I told him I'd been working on my meditation skills. He'd heard this from me about a thousand times before, so, being a pretty practical and direct guy, he said "Well, let's see if all that meditation is working for you." I nervously replied with, "OK," and he proceeded to ask me a "psychic" question: name a person he worked with at his job. Immediately, I tensed and felt anxious and nervous about getting it wrong. My brain started swimming, and I blurted out the first name that came into my head: "Cassandra!" Lawrence responded enthusiastically, excitedly telling me that Cassandra was the name of his boss's daughter. She'd recently been spending a lot of time at their office and hanging out with him and his coworkers.

Impressed, he then suggested I give his coworker a psychic reading. A reading?! I responded, "I'm in no position to be giving anyone a reading. I'm not a professional reader, and I haven't had any training. I don't even know how I would structure the reading to be able to give any useful information." He persisted and put his coworker on the phone right there for a session. Maybe I was in a state of shock because of how quickly I'd gone *that day* from meditating to practicing. But, I did it that moment–I completed my first reading.

It was like riding a high. After her reading, she told a friend, who told another, who told another. Within weeks, I was booked and busy doing free readings for folks. I remember coming home one evening from my after-school part-time job to my mom, confused as to why I was getting so many calls from strangers. I told her what I had been doing, and she remarked that the phone was starting to ring all the time with people asking if they could receive a reading. Yes, this was still the era of the landline. The experience was insane and humbling at the same time.

That psychic growth spurt lasted for a few months. Then, I ran into a couple of challenging clients. The first was an older gentleman who was a local practicing psychic brujo, the Spanish word for witch, and a spell caster. He wanted to see what all the hype was about. Just knowing this man was a "professional" threw my mind into a fit of nervousness and self-doubt. The read was okay, but it was pretty obvious I was struggling to sense detail. He comforted me about how I did, letting me know it was understandable that I was struggling–he also let me know I didn't live up to his expectations. He told me that my abilities didn't compare to his but suggested I keep trying to develop my skills; if I was serious about my craft, I could seek him out as my teacher. My flow was interrupted, and I struggled mentally for days replaying my interaction with him. With other clients, giving readings became labored, like I was pulling teeth to accurately come up with information.

After a few days of recovering my ego, I found my flow again. I soon did another reading for a young guy that heard about me. When I was reading for him, I saw a visceral scene in my mind showing prison doors closing and heard metal doors slamming. It felt directly relevant to him, so I advised him to be cautious about his associations, as he could risk legal trouble if he wasn't mindful of the company he kept. To put it mildly, he did not receive this information well and began to argue with me, insulting me personally. He said that I obviously didn't know anything about anyone and was WRONG! He claimed I was a fraud and that nothing I ever said was correct to anyone, ever! His words cut me down, making me feel like I was still a teenager without the wisdom necessary to evaluate my actions. I could not collect myself enough to formulate a response and did not feel confident enough to defend myself, my integrity, or my work.

He was wrong, of course, but I was shook. I tried to take the criticism with grace, but I could not stop fixating on why this stranger would "come for me" on such a personal level in such an aggressive manner. His words definitely hit me deeply and echoed criticism I'd already received from my own family and friends. After the call, I sat in the living room and spoke to God. If people were going to be this cruel to me, and if I'm not going to be 100% accurate, I don't want to do this work.

My resolution was to stop doing readings. Although I was still doing readings for free, I felt like I could not trust myself anymore to be playing with giving out my services at all. That sentiment proved prophetic. In the ensuing days, I felt a shift in my psychic abilities. The shift would continue for weeks and, eventually, years. My ability to accurately perceive was clouded by my self-doubt and lack of self-worth.

At worst, I began to lose touch with my natural empathetic sensing ability. Before I'd started practicing with readings, I'd used empathy to survive, picking up on the feelings and thoughts of others to help me figure out the best response to any situation. This skill helped me survive the years of abuse as a child when my stepfather's emotions could be the difference between peace and a beating. It helped me with bullies in school and to connect with my more open classmates to find a place of security. But, after I affirmed my choice to God, my sensing abilities stopped. I doubted I'd ever experience them again.

The psychic block of my own making lasted ten years.

Renaissance of Psychic Ferny – Trigger & Reactivation

Still, throughout my 20s, I'd try to reinvigorate my psychic abilities. With the reduction of my empathic ability, I didn't feel like myself anymore. I felt disconnected from the rest of the world and unable to understand other people's emotional positions. I felt depressed and lacked connection.

A lot was happening at home as well. My mother, who had been battling schizophrenia off and on for years, was cycling back into an unstable mental period. The medications she was prescribed turned her into a zombie, and she spent most of her days asleep in bed. My younger and middle sister Irene had also come to live with us. Irene had also begun to suffer from hormone-fueled teenage identity crises, manifested by manic moods and extreme depression.

I was in my first year of community college at the time, struggling to balance my aspirations and my responsibility to them. I began to wonder if I, too, suffered from mental illness and sought a doctor. The doctor listened to me and made a general diagnosis, prescribing me antidepressants.

Medications can prove to be beneficial for some to treat mental illness, but they did not work for me. The medication only amplified my sense of detachment and lack of connection. I stopped feeling anything emotionally. What little sensing ability I had left was gone, and I became a stranger to myself. After a few months, I decided I needed to deal with my challenges differently and stopped taking the medication. I took a job at Starbucks as a barista. New friendships and activities began to fill the holes in my life. One person I met in the drive-thru would prove to change my life and place me back on my proper trajectory.

Her name was...let's just call her Karen with a HARD K...a massage therapist and aspiring Reiki healer. I'd never heard of Reiki, but I was enraptured by Karen's spiritual mindset and outlook on life. Our connection seemed to transcend space and time, and we grew close over the next few years.

I had hit a brick wall with deciding on my future career path, and I had already purchased and read countless books on psychic development and shuffled through various tarot cards and oracle decks. Sometimes, while playing with the decks, the cards would speak to me, but I would shrug off their suggestions, unable to trust myself. With my belief that there had been no change to my psychic ability, I decided that I had nothing to lose. After many attempts, I finally agreed to take Karen's Reiki certification course.

Sure, I was good with my coffee job, but it was not what I wanted to do with my life. The blockage, however, had made me almost abandon my dream of being a professional psychic and medium. I wanted my own business, to be my own boss, to work my own hours, to design my own future, and to choose who I gave my energy to. I was not going to accomplish any of this by working at Starbucks. By taking Karen's course, I could at least move *toward* my goals–formulate an exit strategy–while working as an energy healer. I wanted whatever freedom I could sustain, and as the blockage persisted, Reiki offered me a way to gain satisfaction by helping others heal.

At this point, Karen had converted most of her massage clients into her Reiki services and wanted to grow her clientele base beyond that. I was still working at Starbucks, had been promoted to Assistant Store Manager, and was actively training for my next role as Store Manager. Starbucks provided training in marketing and advertising strategies, so when Karen asked, I was more than eager to pitch ideas to help her grow her practice. This was the era of the Groupon deal, and I proposed that Karen begin offering her services on Groupon. Although she'd take an initial loss by offering her services at a discount, it would give her exposure to a larger number of people, and the potential for repeat customers would be a benefit for her business. When her business started to boom, she took me on as a Reiki practitioner.

Reiki means "universal life energy," and the practice originated in Japan as a way to support physical, emotional, and spiritual well-being by channeling healing energy through the hands. As a Reiki practitioner, my goal was to tap into my clients' energy and help them find balance, realigning them by channeling the connection between them and the universe. I wanted so badly to be of help to my clients. As I began to take appointments and practice my skills, I quickly discovered something was off, and customer feedback reflected the same. I couldn't figure out what I was doing wrong. I knew the principles, I was diligent in my training, I discussed practices with others in the community, I activated the Reiki symbols, and I took care to ground myself before each session. This intentional alignment with the Earth helped stabilize my energy and prevent transferring it to the client. Even though my knowledge and dedication impressed my peers, nothing significantly improved my outcomes with clients.

Venting my frustrations on this Reiki-related blockage to Karen provided some clarity. She asked me about my methodology. In detail, I revealed each step of my process. From my response, she knew the problem. It was not that I was practicing *wrong*. My technique was right, meticulous even. Even the best technique couldn't fix my mindset. My desire to succeed and forge my own path while helping others led me, either consciously or subconsciously, to put immense pressure on myself to be the next miracle worker aka the Jesus Christ Superstar of Reiki. In my sessions, my mind held fast to the idea and left me without the balance I tried so sincerely to give my clients.

I was experiencing a "control freak" blockage and an "ego" blockage, both forms of self-blockage. Furthermore, my seeming inability to get the right results in my clients formed a doubt blockage. Instead of surrendering to the flow of energy during the Reiki process, I focused my energy on being a Super Healer and tried to dictate the outcome of the session so it would match my ego. I expected that, with a series of preordained steps, I would be able to perform Reiki perfectly and obtain predictable results. When I finally realized what was happening, I knew I needed to adjust my mindset instead of adding more items to my routine. I needed to be flexible with the process and forgiving toward myself.

By practicing trust and faith in the process, in my skills, and in the connection with my clients, I finally found myself endeavoring to *experience* Reiki instead of controlling it. That shift was crucial. My sessions went from lackluster to excellent, leading to positive feedback, returning clients, and word-of-mouth new client referrals. For the first time in a long time, I felt myself connecting with people again, sensing things empathetically about my clients, and adjusting my practice to meet their needs, not to meet my needs.

The more I practiced, the stronger my senses became. My hands would move over a client's body, and I would pick up on details related to traumas in their lives. Working on different areas of their energy would garner more information, and what I was learning would become increasingly specific. By surrendering to the process of channeling energy, I released control, ego, and doubt. A switch flipped. I knew this was the moment I'd hoped for. I'd beaten the block, and it was time to reunite with my psychic sensing ability.

As the breakthroughs continued, I regained my confidence. Eventually, I left with the goal of creating my own practice. It was difficult at first. I changed locations many times and ultimately worked from my own home. I had to dodge the shady people in the spiritual business community who wanted to prey on talent, either by exploiting it or eradicating it, to feed their egos and wallets. Through all the negativity, I kept that faith in myself. I learned to accept myself where I was while keeping my vision for the future in mind. With my business came a new sense of satisfaction and, through my work, a new sense of fulfillment.

My block was banished. I was truly *back in business.*

CHAPTER 8

Precognition: Why I Haven't Won the Lottery

L ife is a game of chance, so why can't psychics rig the odds in their favor?

If a psychic can have visions about major world events and can see into others' futures, why can't they just focus on lottery numbers and never have to work again? Here's the truth: like everyone, I want to win the lottery. Sure, I would do some good with the money–build a new center for LBGTQIA+ kids from my hometown to find a space for community, give to Planned Parenthood to protect the right to choose, or donate to my local food bank–but I would also love to be free from worrying about the financial stability of myself and my loved ones. That is *exactly* why I can't see those lottery numbers.

Precognition is the ability to perceive future events and outcomes through psi sensing. Precognitive experiences usually arrive through intuitive impressions–our instincts–or through our dreams. The first part of precognition requires expertly filtering out psi information to home in on what is most pertinent. The second part of precognition, as is true with all psychic sensing, is the ability to interpret the information received accurately.

As a universal rule, we can't accurately see what happens to ourselves. If we try to tune into our own futures, we activate the part of our minds aligned with achieving a certain goal or outcome. It's natural to dream of achieving future goals. Especially for those who wish to escape their present circumstances, sometimes the dream is what allows them to get through the day. But this habit of imagining living in your idealized future today blocks you from making accurate predictions about your future.

Accurate interpretation requires recognizing the biases that may color our perception. We can't accurately see our futures (without significant practice) because we are *biased* in favor of ourselves. This chapter is dedicated to draining the color of bias to sharpen our psychic acumen.

With the Wind in Your Sails – How We Begin to Change

We, as humans trapped in loops of routine, typically run on autopilot, propelled by the momentum of our normal thought patterns. These thought patterns carry us forward with a predictable consistency. Think of a human being as a gigantic boat moving toward the shore: we move slowly, large, heavy, uneasy to redirect, barreling forward with reaching the shore as the only consideration.

Imagine that we, the gigantic boat, have a tiny sail. The boat has an intended path, but to get there, it must learn how to maneuver through the waters with the aid of the wind. Wind may be gusting, forceful, and impossible to ignore. Wind may be dramatically shifting, effortlessly tossing those in its way. Wind may be gentle, slight, almost imperceptible: a slight puff in the sail pushing us *a liiiitle* off our path. Without the wind, we bob in the water, unable to assert any directionality. So, we learn, painstakingly, to listen to each perceptible wisp and to watch how they interact with each other and with our sail. We cannot be on autopilot and reach our destination. Our focus must be rapt. We may not reach the point on shore we initially had in mind, but we gain valuable information along the way. In practice, we are mere servants to the universe, and we must let ourselves be used as the vessel regardless of where it takes us.

Improving the power of our sails requires strong psychic muscles, and strong psychic muscles come from increasing awareness through meditation. The more sensitive we become to forces outside of ourselves, the easier our sails pick up on the right winds, countering the currents seeking to lead us astray. We build momentum over time, able to receive more information through our clair senses, becoming highly conductive beacons for receiving psychic information and expertly interpreting the energy received.

Even with decades of practicing honing your psychic skills, it is unlikely that you will be able to fully overcome the barrier of wanting your idealized future. That lottery jackpot is a goal, represented by the port you're aiming for on the shore. You can't navigate there because your desire clouds the path. With time and skill, you can *better* learn how to navigate through the fog of your desires by catching gusts of energy with your sails.

In this extended metaphor, the sails are your intuition. Intuitive sensing is picking up on the energy around you while simultaneously being able to interpret what that energy means. Broadly speaking, intuition is the first or "weakest" level of psychic sensing. Intuition does not provide you with a clear path; however, it provides you with an inkling, letting an inference guide you, albeit in a murkier way than the conscious awareness that accompanies deeper psychic sensing. With practice, though, intuitive sensing significantly sharpens.

Seeking control over the destination is the death of intuition because you've already determined where what you're feeling will bring you–the energy is interpreted within your expectations. By shifting our focus from the hope of reaching a destination to the minutiae of the process, we can begin to truly sense, letting even the most minuscule changes in energy guide our intuition. With the navigation tools of memory recall or remote viewing, we can learn how to steer. Meditation can help us see, allowing clarity through the fog.

In all this, we may pick up numbers on the way. The sails of our intuitions can still guide us. The numbers could be a date. Perhaps they're an address. Maybe they're a flight number. They may well be lottery numbers, too, but probably not for the lottery you played.

Okay, But I Also Dreamed I Won the Lottery!

I see you, clever little thing! If it's not a conscious desire, can I access those sweet, sweet numbers through a different form of psychic sensing? I would love to say yes, but the answer is no. At its heart, the problem is that when we *dream* about our futures, we're using the same parts of our mind that we use to psychically sense. The memory centers we use to envision something in our mind's eye to start the sensing process…seem a lot like the images we conjure up in our fantasies. The image our fantasies create is stored by the mind. We are too close to ourselves to separate the dream from the sensing. When we work with (most) clients, we are far enough removed that we have perspective and aren't seeing images through the lens of what we *hope* to see.

Have you ever closed your eyes and, maybe, imagined that the book you were writing is finished? You feel all warm and fuzzy only to wake to a cursor blinking on a blank page? You feel the progress although nothing more is written.

That sensation symbolizes the blending of fact and fiction with our desires, which obscures our ability to accurately perceive our future. Whether consciously or unconsciously, we're activating the same components in our brain that we use to dream.

For those that are destined to win: you might just dream about it before it happens. And this *does* happen. Timothy Schultz had a dream about winning the Powerball in 1999 before taking home the $29 million jackpot. Cynthia Stafford visualized herself winning $112 million, taking home that same amount in 2007. Maybe they used techniques to bring the lottery to them. In cases like these, I believe the lottery was already their destiny, and their will merely aligned with the outcome.

So, for a majority of the population, don't bet on winning that jackpot just because you dreamed it!

FERNANDO MARRON

A Dream of Bias

A client once came to me with a dream they wanted to be interpreted.

She'd had a dream where she was in her home but uneasy because she felt as if it was about to be broken into. In her dream, the person outside her home was Black, leading her to develop a wariness of Black men in real life, despite having no prior trauma associated with them.

This was in the middle of the Black Lives Matter resurgence in 2020. At the time, I was doing a lot of work on myself and countering my biases. Using my knowledge, I tried to figure out her biases to determine why she'd had this dream.

As we talked, I found we shared many similar background traits: we were similar in age, Hispanic, and grew up in poorer communities in Texas. I related to her experience because I grew up in Houston, Texas, in the 80s and 90s. The city was (and still is) incredibly diverse demographically but severely segregated geographically. Asians had Chinatown. Whites lived in the suburbs. The Black areas were intersected by the highway. And we, the Hispanics, filled in the gaps between other ethnic groups, yet remained segregated among ourselves by social class.

We grew up poor, but when we got off the highway, my *tia* instinctively locked our doors so fast as we drove through Black neighborhoods–like we needed to act like we had something they didn't. This hypervigilance was fed to me through a diet of racism informed by fear. It had no basis in reality. Our neighborhood wasn't any "nicer." It just looked like us.

In her entire life, Black men never posed a threat to my client. So why, now, was she being haunted by this dream of a Black man walking by her window? He wasn't doing anything. He wasn't hurting her. He wasn't even real.

Her dream wasn't prophetic. It wasn't trying to tell her something that was going to happen. The dream was her unconscious mind's way of remaining fearful of Black men, now in the context of them marching on her street, destroying her home, and taking her property. The threat from her childhood now mutated to attack those things she'd acquired to distance herself from her childhood.

This woman came to me because she was embarrassed and wanted to free herself from this guilt. I told her that I could not free her. I told her that she needed to confront the beliefs she had been taught in order to free herself. I told her that she needed to learn a new way to relate with and empathize with those different from her.

Her racist biases clouded her ability to see the dream for what it was: a manifestation of her anxiety about the racist beliefs she held— beliefs she held magnified by the Black Lives Matter movement and right-wing propaganda. She didn't aim to get rid of the dream; she wanted to know what it meant. In that, she was refusing to deal with the racism at the heart of the matter. Just like with this individual, a bias in the self will lead to a bias in interpretation, whether that be in the interpretation of a dream or interpretation in psychic sensing. The more you can separate yourself from the bias, the better your interpretive abilities will become.

You *must* deal with your bullshit. If you can't confront your biases or determine how they've shaped you, then you'll continue to be blocked by them. Your capacity for empathy will be limited because there will always be a barrier between you and the life of someone not like you. Communication with others and with yourself is key.

Biases in Interpretation

While we've primarily discussed self-bias, my experiences have led me to identify three levels of objectivity that influence how we sense and interpret psychic information:

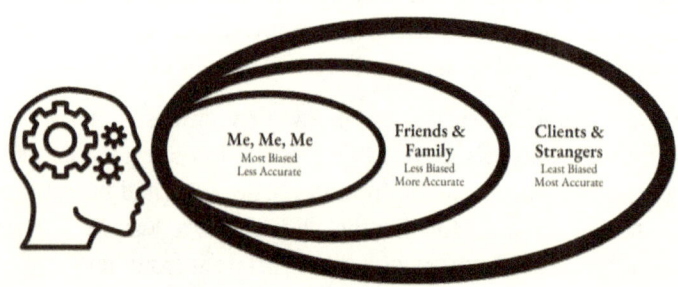

1) Strangers/(Most) Clients

"Where the relationship is lean, the reading is clean."

Whereas we find it difficult to interpret for ourselves because of our wishes and desires, it is easiest to interpret where we lack a relationship with the individual. We are largely uninvested in the intricacies of the lives of strangers. We may wish them well in a general sense, but we do not know about their relationship with their sister, so we cannot hope for that relationship to be repaired in the future.

During a reading, then, we can interpret what we're seeing as devoid of extra information or emotional baggage. We don't feel affected by their reaction to the information in the reading. We aren't as worried about their response. They'll either accept it or not. They'll either go their separate ways or come back for another visit. Que será será.

One of my very first professional gigs was in Houston as a reader at a local bookstore's "Psychic Sunday." I'd quickly lined up a full day of bookings and started with my readings. I was getting lots of positive feedback, leaving people amazed with how much I could tell them. Even when the reading revealed less-than-positive information, the people were still pleased. A woman even thanked me because she was tired of psychics constantly telling her what they thought she wanted to hear, grateful for being honest and direct about my sensing.

My confidence was good. I was doing good!

Then, my next appointment arrived. She walked up to my table like she could smell that someone was feeling good about themselves, and she followed that scent to tear them down. This woman heard I was good from a friend, and she opened. Already, it felt like a challenge–an attempt at intimidation. Now, I   might be more hesitant around someone approaching me with that negative energy, but back then, I was just starting out, building muscle, and eager to do as much reading as I possibly could.

She sat down, put her cheap purse on the floor, and crossed her arms. I took my cards out. After shuffling, I attempted to sense things about her life. Before I could speak, she lost her patience and said, "Tell me something already." My ability froze. As I was working through that blockage, she began to ask me questions instead. She was writing a book, of course, and she wanted to know how it was going to go, about her future writing deal, and the millions in royalties that went with it. From her phrasing, the only acceptable answer for her was "New York Times Bestseller" with endless fame and fortune. But that's not what I saw. I told her the truth, "I don't feel confident your book is going to achieve the level of success you're aiming for–you may not even finish writing it–so it's not going to make you a millionaire, and it's not going to make you famous." Oop.

She had also inquired about her love life. The stars in her eyes told me that she had someone in mind and sought good news. Already unhappy with the book reveal, her face curled into a scowl as I dealt the cards.

"Well, I don't feel that the guy moving to Houston to be with you is your soulmate."

Her eyebrows furrowed so deeply they nearly connected.

"In fact, I think there may be someone else in the picture that's going to be an obstacle in the relationship and will impact the move of the guy you're asking about."

Her eyes glazed over.

"Actually, I think you may be the one with someone else."

In real time, I saw the words leave my lips, float into her ears, hit her brain, and turn her face pink.

Now, she was finished with me. She scoffed. Every psychic she'd been to had confirmed that he was her soulmate. They all told her she'd be having a happily ever after. Only I dared to doubt their love. Only I had the audacity to question her fidelity. Yes, she did have an additional little someone on the side, but that wasn't what she was asking about. It was too much for her.

She trashed me to the owner of the bookstore–that same friend that raved to her about me–and, unsurprisingly, I wasn't invited back for Psychic Sunday. While saddened by losing this opportunity, I still felt great about the readings I did for the people willing to accept the multifaceted nature of the truth. From that gig, I still made connections and had people seek me out afterwards for my services. Accuracy, not flattery.

2) Friends/Family/Frequent Clients

"When you care, you'll want to be there. In a reading, that's not fair."

Your friends and family are people whose lives you've invested in. Your frequent clients are people whose lives you've witnessed develop, feeling like you've been beside them for as long as you've been on the ride.

You want to see your friend Erica find someone who truly deserves her. You feel this because, through countless conversations with Erica, you've witnessed her heartbreak, and you've heard her yearn to find someone who will cherish her for who she is.

You want your sister to be able to afford the big house on the corner that's only half a mile from you. Every time you and she drive by the house, she tugs on your sleeve or squeezes your shoulder excitedly squealing, "One day!" It's cute, and you love her.

Monica comes for a reading every Thursday. You've seen her patterns and know, before she opens her mouth, what type of person is causing her grief. Tall, dark, and emotionally unavailable. You feel like you could even tune out because she is *so* predictable.

3) Your Self

"With clouds of want, I can't see clearly, so the aims of my readings I'll miss dearly."

It's not a secret. I'd love to win the lottery. I'd love to spread my knowledge on psychic sensing to the world and empower others to believe in themselves. Absolutely. And for that reason, I can't see my future clearly. I can clear up some of the fog, trusting the wind in my tiny sail, using surrounding energy to inform my intuition. But accuracy is not guaranteed to follow.[19]

We act, whether consciously or unconsciously, guided by this self-bias. It guides our thoughts, emotions, and behaviors. We make decisions based on how to best secure our future and use our energy. With these biases ingrained in everything we do, it's logical that these are most difficult to avoid.

Whatever you do, *don't* seek validation through your readings. Your worth as a person and as a psychic is not dependent on how close your readings are to actuality. As a psychic, you can always improve. As a person, you are inherently worthy. Also, as a person, you are inherently psychic, so be kind and patient with yourself. Make room for error. Room for error is room for growth.

---

[19] In the same vein, if you seek fame, then your readings will be skewed by the desire to be as big as possible, not as accurate as possible.

I've had amateur psychics come to me who claim they "sense futures precisely" and "are never inaccurate." Hate to say it, but, respectfully, you can't and you aren't. These psychics will come to me for a reading so they may "confirm" the futures they've predicted for themselves, not because they fear immaturity in their abilities.

One such person had her world upended after she based future decisions on a vision she received and misinterpreted. She was a fellow intuitive with her own energy practice. By all accounts, she was a success. Then, one day during a meditation, she received a vision of a bunch of chairs dancing in a circle. On the back of one chair was the image of a fish. In the vision, she entered the circle and sat on the fish chair. The fish chair stopped dancing.

At the time, she was infatuated with a lady cop who loved fishing. Insecure and desperate to be with this woman, she spun the vision in a way that suited her delusions. The chair rested because it found a home with her. The chair represented the object of her desire because of the fish. The dancing was a courting ritual. So, the vision meant that she and her lady love would soon be one.

If she'd trusted her intuition instead of attempting to bend it to her will, she would have realized it was trying to tell her something far simpler. She was a serial dater, constantly flitting from one person to the next. She'd fixate on the object of her desire, they'd eventually reject her, and she'd move on to the next. The musical chairs were *her* love life, and it was telling her to find a new chair.

In real life, she ended up *moving*, uprooting her entire life, and giving up her practice, for this lady cop who ended up rejecting her. Her entire world collapsed. Even though she still practices, she's nowhere near her previous heights of success. Last I heard, she's living in a Tiny House in Oklahoma.

I don't mean that you can never read for yourself. I just wouldn't bet on it.

Compartmentalizing With Compassion

Sensitivity is one of the most important skills in any psychic reading. When someone is close to you, there's too much sensitivity already there; therefore, to get an accurate reading, you must figure out how to contain your biases. This is not to say to turn off your sensitivity, but you must figure out how to turn it down when trying to accurately read those you know well. You must also figure out how to turn down your knowledge about them to prevent what you already know from impacting your reading and interpretation.

Even in readings with strangers, you must limit your personal attachment to retain an accurate reading. When a client is seeking information on a topic where you carry trauma, it can cause your judgment and unresolved issues to cloud your reading, imparting too much of yourself onto the client. You start to feel a sense of duty. You try to give them the lessons you've learned, sharing information based on your own life. By this point, you're invested too deeply in their outcome. Too biased to provide accurate readings, you instead offer advice, hoping to change their fortunes in a way you couldn't achieve for yourself. You're now a life coach.

I've seen so many instances of psychics giving terrible relationship advice to their clients because the client's romantic interest exhibited behavior that triggered their past trauma. Instead of remaining objective, the unprocessed trauma overshadows the sensed details, creating assumptions, and interlacing the client's interest with the psychic's.

I have been guilty of this too. I had to confront my unprocessed trauma from past abuse to prevent it from hijacking my readings, particularly when it came to working with hypermasculine men. In my discussion of blockages, I mentioned that I stopped doing readings for a time after a man went off on me. Even though I'd never met this man, his voice told me, "big, tough, masculine." Already in a vulnerable state to remain open during the reading, hearing that voice brought me back to being a child. I remembered all the men that would hurt me, tease me, or make me fear–and I was triggered. In service to this guy that might be going to prison, I tried my best to put my feelings aside and do the reading. Being vulnerable in that space was difficult, but I managed to overcome my hesitation to try to connect with him. He, however, was nasty to me. I guess the women who convinced him to try a psychic forgot to remind him of the rules for basic human interactions. It ended up making my hesitation about reading for straight men worse for years–something I've recently overcome.

Why did so many psychics predict Hillary Clinton would win the 2016 election? A large percentage of the population, including psychics, could not conceive a world where the perpetually unserious and virulently racist, sexist, ableist, ageist, homophobic, xenophobic, islamophobic, etc. candidate with no political experience would win over the perpetually competent Hillary Clinton. Plus, many psychics especially saw and felt an opportunity for the first female president, so the alternative was unfathomable. The personal investment in Hillary and disgust for Trump led to inaccurate predictions.

Compartmentalization can minimize (not eliminate) the effects of biases on the psychic senses.

Compartmentalization involves splitting the personal from the incipient task, accommodating detachment from the outcome of the reading. Put simply, compartmentalization is *boundaries*. There needs to be a limit to how much of your "self" you insert into readings. Through this, you can read for strangers without being affected by your trauma or fear of their reaction to the information. You can also sense better for family and friends. You may even become better at sensing for yourself–you've been warned about that, though.

Dissociation is the best way I can describe effective compartmentalization. It is like operating a vehicle without the driver–the car moves, but the person stays still. I still have to use emotions when sensing, but I avoid being pulled into the outcome. I engage with the separation, empowering myself to put aside my reactions until the reading is over. As a child, I needed to separate myself from my emotions to survive. In being forced to remove myself from the reality of the situation, I avoided descending into personal madness or into the chaos of the surrounding situation. This is the same method I use to compartmentalize today.

I am still a person who permits myself to sense all the energy in the room during a reading for the benefit of accuracy. After a reading, though, I may think about what happened and take a private moment to feel. In a way, it is almost liberating in moments during the reading to know that I can separate my "self" from the sensing. Addressing my trauma and removing the need to people please gives me the ability to assert these boundaries.

For a time, readings in person were hard for me because I would feel overwhelmed by the depth of connection. After COVID forced us all online, I grew to find that being virtual allowed me greater disconnection from the emotional weight of a reading. I no longer felt the heat of their eyes on me as I contemplated in silence, avoiding the excess energy of their feedback. When in-person meetings resumed, the skills I learned from being able to read through a screen proved valuable when protecting myself from vicarious trauma in-person. Now, most of my sessions are virtual, preserving more bandwidth for the occasional in-person sessions. That's my boundary.

In the absence of compartmentalization, psychics who lack boundaries will frequently find themselves overwhelmed by the weight of the work and absorb others' trauma. This hinders them from engaging full-time in psychic practice. Working on yourself is an asset in the psychic's toolkit.

How to Separate Specialization from Bias

Remember the postman who was able to sense numbers and addresses more easily because he'd delivered mail to hundreds of thousands of people? That's not a bias. That's a specialization. A specialization is a *skill* that one strengthens, like a muscle, bias is inherently present. The specialization is reading a textbook; the bias is studying your margin notes. Use the skills you possess without substituting your interpretation, and you can take advantage of your skills without succumbing to your biases.

Use past experiences to inform your readings, not your present ego.

During readings, I make sure that I share everything that I'm sensing so my clients can see where I'm coming from. I always make sure they know that I am looking at pieces, not home movies, so they don't take everything I say as gospel. Even if my interpretation is off, I encourage them to remain open to the message. While my interpretation of the details may not be exact, the details themselves are still accurate and may reflect the bigger picture. Not only does that help provide focus during the reading, it builds trust between the client and me. Reading is a process connecting two people–the client and the conduit–so it should be a collaboration: your skill + your sensitivity + your experience + your specialization + their contexts.

Chelsea – How Biases Can Be Dangerous

I have a cautionary tale to tell.

Several years ago, I conducted a reading for my friend, Chelsea. Chelsea was bright and effervescent. She had a free spirit and was mature far beyond her years. She was able to see things more clearly than most people. Her charisma was distinct and her affect, warm. I met her when she was on a spiritual journey, diving into texts and materials that I wouldn't touch until my late twenties. At the time, aside from being her boss as her store manager at Starbucks, I'd become her spiritual guide, eager to lift this bright light to great heights.

At the time, I thought our psychic abilities worked the same in every reading. When I sought information about a topic, all I needed to do was focus on it, and I would instinctively arrive at the answer. The subject of the reading could not affect the journey to the answer, I thought. I approached readings with family as I did with clients and friends, ignorant of the levels of objectivity at play in each situation.

Chelsea lived only a few blocks from me, so we would spend time together. Through her studies, she piqued an interest in having tarot readings. Knowing my experience with tarot, she asked if I could do a reading for her. I did not hesitate to say yes, gathering my cards almost as immediately as she made the request. This would just be another summer day of Chelsea and I deepening our connection, or so I thought.

In the session, I had a very intense vision where Chelsea's mother was sitting in a chair in what appeared to be a hospital room, looking positively devastated. The vibe was that of a family saddened, perhaps by the weight of grief. In interpreting the vision, I could never conceive it related to Chelsea–it featured her mom, so I felt guided to the conclusion that the subject *was* her mom. I believed this vision was trying to tell me that there was an impending burden, illness, or death in the family later that year. Still, I tried to stay light. I told Chelsea to focus on her mother's health and get her to the doctor as fast as she could. In doing so, I hoped to spare the family from the agony of loss so close to the holidays.

A few months later, on December 1st, 2013, Chelsea left her workplace at Whole Foods late, around 10:25 P.M., and headed home. Chelsea was riding her bike when she was hit from behind by a drunk driver in a truck. The driver did not stop, leaving Chelsea on the side of the road in the middle of the night. Eventually, a good Samaritan came across her and called 911. This person cradled Chelsea until the paramedics arrived on the scene.

On the morning of December 2nd, I received a text on my phone from a group chat started by one of Chelsea's closest friends. The message shocked me. Chelsea was in a coma. We didn't get more information than that, and we waited for more details. Later that day, I visited her in the hospital. As I approached her family in the waiting area of the ICU, I saw her mother, sitting in a hospital chair, looking distraught. The vision from months prior raced back, bowling me over with its details. I knew that the prognosis would not be good, and I had interpreted my vision incorrectly. Chelsea's mom wasn't in danger. The vision was about Chelsea.

A few days later, Chelsea passed away. I spiraled. I felt guilty and inadequate alongside intense grieving. Replaying the vision in my head, I chastised myself for what I failed to see. How could someone so young and close to me with such a bright future meet such an untimely end? Could I have prevented her death? Could I have warned her? Why did I mess up? Awash in a reservoir of self-doubt, I blamed myself, I cursed my skills, and I dissected every moment to find my mistakes.

My love and admiration for Chelsea blinded me to the truth of my vision. I could not bear the thought of losing Chelsea, so I interpreted what I saw favorably to prevent that outcome. My biases rerouted my perception away from what my heart could not bear to know. If I couldn't see it, it wouldn't happen. The details of my vision were still relevant, but I ignored the feeling in my gut that I needed to explore other possibilities because of my biases.

Through the harsh relief of a newspaper heading, I learned the truth of psychic readings: they are only as accurate as the reader's ability to remain objective, and the reader is only consistently accurate once they can overcome their biases. I now knew the importance of objectivity.

Shortly after Chelsea's passing, her sister informed me that Chelsea told them about my prediction. Chelsea really had faith in my psychic abilities and spiritual wisdom.

That was an emotional kick-in-the-ass. It moved me to take my work as a psychic medium more seriously. Chelsea is the reason why I started my business full-time that year. It is in her memory that I do this work.

Compartmentalization Does Not Need to be Amputation

TRANSPORTATION

Mayra Beltrán photos / Houston Chronicle

Fernando Marron leaves remembrances at the memorial for Chelsea Norman, a cyclist who was hit and killed by a motorist.

'Ghost bike' honors a young life

Hundreds of riders to converge on the area to press authorities to enforce rules of road

By Dane Schiller

They call it the "ghost bike." It is painted completely white, even the tires, and chained to a street post in Montrose.

The shrine near West Gray and Waugh marks where cyclist Chelsea Norman was hit 10 days ago by a motorist and later died of her injuries.

There are no known witnesses. The driver fled. Exactly what happened remains a mystery that police and Norman's family continue to probe.

The bike is flanked by candles and flowers to honor the 24-year-old who was riding home at about 10:25 p.m. from her job a few blocks away at Whole Foods Market.

The spot has quickly become sacred ground. Tears are shed. Memories are shared. It is also a rallying point for cyclists calling for more safety among their own ranks as well as denouncing motorists who they say drive with impunity from the law and disdain for sharing the road.

Hundreds of riders are expected to converge on the area at 7 p.m. Wednesday to remind Houston of the Dec. 1 incident and pressure authorities to reduce the chances of it happening again by enforcing laws and enhancing bike paths.

Among the riders who vows to be there is Fred Zapalac, co-owner of the Blue Line Bike Lab bike shops.

"I would say the cycling community is by and large very angry," he said. "This beautiful 24-year-old girl that was struck down and killed has really lit a fire under people. I think anybody that knows anybody who rides a bike in this city would be very concerned about this — and anybody who has a heart."

Cyclists continues on B2

Chelsea L. Norman

Friends and family gather for the memorial service of Chelsea Norman, 24.

I can feel the heat of a candle in the moment, touch the flame, and feel pain, but that doesn't mean I need to go out and destroy all the candles in the grocery store. During a reading, it's essential to allow yourself to feel, engage, and be present in the experience without attaching a deeper narrative to any single moment.

When reading, you move from one moment of experience to the next. The danger comes when you combine the moment with a desire or interpret it through judgment. If you feel pain during a reading–and even with practice at compartmentalizing, this can happen–it's important to identify, acknowledge, and understand that pain. Why is this coming up? What does it mean in the context of this reading? How can it help me better understand the situation of this client? Is a pattern presenting? Is there another association? Acknowledge the emotion, detach from it, and analyze it to find its purpose. If such a strong reaction comes up in a reading despite practiced compartmentalization, there may be a reason.

But the biggest key to compartmentalization: STOP GIVING A SHIT!

Yes, your job requires you to be sensitive. But you can turn it off or turn it down. You don't need to be so vulnerable as to invite yourself to be retraumatized to give a good reading. You don't need to tell the client what you think they want to hear to be successful. Present your truth with compassion, but still present the truth. If you lose a client, then it was not meant to be. Strive for honesty, not likeability.

In the end, they'll like you for accurate readings, not for candy-coated delusions that lead to disappointment. The only person that needs to like you, is you. Protect you, protect your peace, and protect your integrity.

When you can love yourself regardless of how others feel, you've already won the lottery.

CHAPTER 9

The Prophetic Dream

It Was More Than Just a Dream...

There I was, standing outside of the White House on a winter night. I watched as a group of Black people began to gather, marching in front of the White House. They reached the gates, and I looked up. Donald Trump stood right in the center of the third-floor balustraded parapet of the southern façade, flanked on each side by an army sharpshooter. Recently removed from power, his access to the historic building was revoked, and he occupied a space from which he was banned. Unfazed, he smiled, his upturned lips and his swollen ego matching the curves of the Truman Balcony below. From his eyes, I knew his mob of MAGA supporters waited in the wings, but I could not determine where. The threat was ominous.

Marcher after marcher began to climb the gates as Trump and his generals menaced from above. One foot at a time, they hoisted themselves over, barricades be damned. With purpose, they continued moving toward the White House. Trump yelled, "SHOOT THEM." But his men failed to move. Then I saw it: Trump turned to his side and grabbed the officer's assault weapon from his hands, finding no resistance, and quickly tipped it downward toward the marchers. That's when he started firing.

Order ceased. This once-organized group of people started running everywhere desperately looking for a safe space to shield themselves from the hail of bullets. Climbing back over the fence, given the lack of visual obstruction, would be a death sentence. I saw an older gentleman from my vantage point, running from the gunfire. As I put my arm out to grab him and pull him to safety, I saw my hand. In this dream, I took the form of a middle-aged Black man. I was one of the marchers. I was a target, too. And as the older man grasped my wrist to let himself be guided by me, he got hit. Again and again. I crouched down, dragging him with both hands to a safe place. He was bloody and bruised, but he was still alive. One of the bullets that hit him grazed me, but I was unharmed except for a black piece of coal lodging itself into my finger. The coal turned into a diamond–it was telling me that something beautiful would have to come out of this horror.

We escaped the area and were rushed to a hospital. Seemingly countless, struck while marching overwhelmed the staff. The old man I was with lived. I did too. But there were so many casualties. The hospital staff's faces grew longer with the hours. Their hands were caked in the blood of tragedy–the visceral ooze of hate. The weight was in the room, and it stayed with us as we left.

My memory skipped from the hospital to outside of a hotel where I worked as a valet and server. A TV visible from the lobby showed images of the massacre that had just unfolded, but the chatter around me was that this horrific event was just a rumor. And that was from the people who even acknowledged the harrowing ordeal—the death of other human beings at the hands of an individual with unchecked power. Between the denials of reality and the experience burned into my soul, the communal posture shook me. As a last gasp, I stood up and started screaming. "THIS IS WHAT HAPPENED. THIS IS REAL."

Then I woke up. It was March 29, 2019, and I began scribbling all of the details of this dream furiously to get as many details as I could before they fell from my memory. As my hands made words, my brain began to interpret, almost like active meditation. The pieces began to fall into place. From what I'd seen, I thought that there would be a march at the Capitol, White House, or another major government building. The march would be helmed by people expressing radical ideas, motivated to act in violence. I thought that, since the people in my dream were Black, it would be Black people involved in the march. People would be hurt or killed during the incident. Although the incident resulted in tremendous pain, my interpretation was that something good would come together in response. Perhaps, I thought, it would result in a stand on a racial issue that would lead to positive change.

This dream deeply conflicted me. I shared my findings with a couple of close friends, seeking their guidance on whether I should share this on social media. Ultimately, I decided that it needed to be made public, so I posted it on Facebook and Instagram. Later, I posted it to my website, https://www.fernandomarron.com/ , posted videos to YouTube, and expanded on the ideas in a medium post.

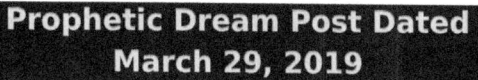

Prophetic Dream Post Dated March 29, 2019

A few months after this dream occurred, George Floyd was killed in Minneapolis, Minnesota, by a white police officer responding to a call of a counterfeit bill. As the murder of George Floyd sparked protests nationwide, uniting a larger group than ever behind the Black Lives Matter movement, the White House encouraged police to use force against protestors. In one show of such authority, Donald Trump had protesters forcefully removed from Lafayette Square using tear gas, riot control, and rubber bullets, so that Trump could walk from the White House to a Church. Trump posed in front of the church, holding up a bible, for a photo op. Two months later,

Kyle Rittenhouse, a Trump supporter and member of the Blue Lives Matter countermovement, took an AR-15 assault rifle to "protect businesses" during a protest against police violence in Wisconsin. He would go on to shoot three men. This felt almost like the dream coming to life.

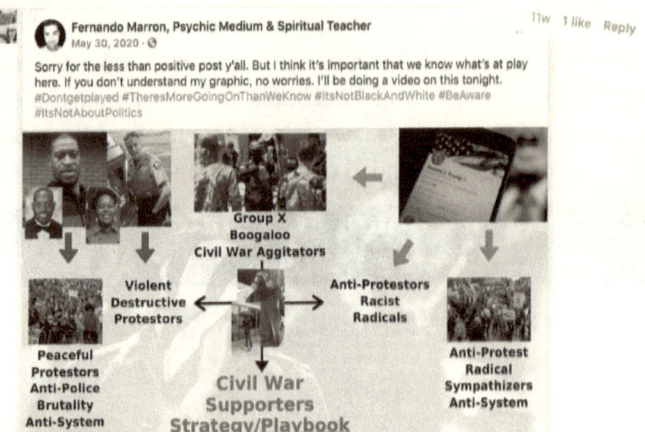

But, even after Trump's June 1, 2020, march on Lafayette Square, I felt that the prophecy was only partially fulfilled. Trump wielded police violence to clear protesters from the Square for a meaningless photo op. This act seemed designed to remind the protestors and the public that he *could* easily quell civil unrest and suppress First Amendment rights as Commander-in-Chief. I felt Trump lose power in my dream, his desperate, Cheeto-stained claws straining to keep their grip over the American people. I felt Trump use his waning power to motivate a destabilization of American Institutions by galvanizing his base to take up arms to defend his legacy.

In November 2020, as the election results rolled in, I knew that the latter part of the prophecy had yet to come to be. With this new context in mind, aspects of the prophetic dream shone in a new light. Issuing an update on my prophetic dream, I warned my followers on social media again to be careful. I wrote that, while Trump took the weapon in my dream, his taking of the weapon did not mean he would shoot himself but, rather, that "many of the people who have become radicalized in their political views and methodology, and are willing to take up arms to fight the president's fight for him" could "take their ability to use assault-style weapons to force change, assume power and make a point to the furthest limits they are allowed to." I did not want to be right, but I felt that I had a duty to try as best I could to keep others safe.

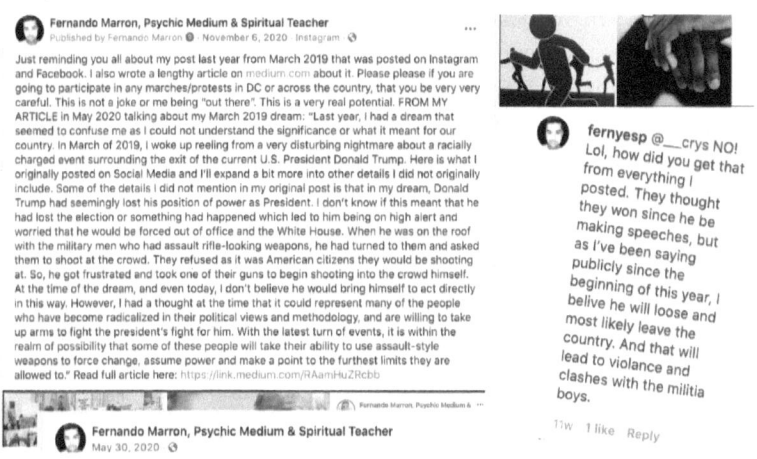

Fernando Marron, Psychic Medium & Spiritual Teacher
Published by Fernando Marron ● · November 6, 2020 · Instagram · ●

Just reminding you all about my post last year from March 2019 that was posted on Instagram and Facebook. I also wrote a lengthy article on medium.com about it. Please please if you are going to participate in any marches/protests in DC or across the country, that you be very very careful. This is not a joke or me being "out there". This is a very real potential. FROM MY ARTICLE in May 2020 talking about my March 2019 dream: "Last year, I had a dream that seemed to confuse me as I could not understand the significance or what it meant for our country. In March of 2019, I woke up reeling from a very disturbing nightmare about a racially charged event surrounding the exit of the current U.S. President Donald Trump. Here is what I originally posted on Social Media and I'll expand a bit more into other details I did not originally include. Some of the details I did not mention in my original post is that in my dream, Donald Trump had seemingly lost his position of power as President. I don't know if this meant that he had lost the election or something had happened which led to him being on high alert and worried that he would be forced out of office and the White House. When he was on the roof with the military men who had assault rifle-looking weapons, he had turned to them and asked them to shoot at the crowd. They refused as it was American citizens they would be shooting at. So, he got frustrated and took one of their guns to begin shooting into the crowd himself. At the time of the dream, and even today, I don't believe he would bring himself to act directly in this way. However, I had a thought at the time that it could represent many of the people who have become radicalized in their political views and methodology, and are willing to take up arms to fight the president's fight for him. With the latest turn of events, it is within the realm of possibility that some of these people will take their ability to use assault-style weapons to force change, assume power and make a point to the furthest limits they are allowed to." Read full article here: https://link.medium.com/RAamHuZRcbb

Fernando Marron, Psychic Medium & Spiritual Teacher
May 30, 2020 · ●

fernyesp @__crys NO! Lol, how did you get that from everything I posted. They thought they won since he be making speeches, but as I've been saying publicly since the beginning of this year, I belive he will loose and most likely leave the country. And that will lead to violence and clashes with the militia boys.

11w   1 like   Reply

And, as predicted, January 6, 2021, arrived. Trump told his Vice President to refuse to certify the Electoral College vote. Trump held a "Save America" rally on the President's South Park to his most fervent followers–Proud Boys, Oath Keepers, and others dedicated to using force to impart their views on others–after his former lackey, Vice President Mike Pence refused to use his power to deny certification of the Electoral College results. Trump, desperate and denying the reality that he'd lost the election, told those gathered to "fight like hell" or else they would "not have a country anymore." And so they did: 2,000 rioters stormed the Capitol, climbed over the gates, and began a plan to forcibly regain control of the legislature. Officers once controlled by Trump lined up to protect the building. Pro-Trump forces, once so pro-police and pro-free speech, fought with Capitol Police and reporters, vandalized congressional offices, and erected a gallows to "Hang Mike Pence." Trump stood by, eventually telling his supporters to "go home in peace." Five died in the 36 hours after the siege of the Capitol. Four additional officers who responded to the attack committed suicide in the next seven months. Over $2.7 million in damage ensued.

When a prophetic dream occurs, it is more like a mishmash of ideas than it is a clear picture of the future. The prophetic dream throws all of the elements of an event into a blender, presses "mince," and produces a concept slurry. Prophetic dreams can require multiple interpretations, reinterpretations, and contextualization based on new facts. In my experience, a single prophetic dream will typically include at least two events occurring contemporaneously or causally linked. Holding a decoder key for the future through a prophetic dream can be overwhelming, but, as shown through my prophetic dream about the George Floyd protests and January 6th, it can also help others.

Once you have a prophetic dream, write it down. Then, take it apart. Inspect each component individually before attempting to interpret the whole. Be open. A prophetic dream will need to be continuously interpreted as time passes–each part may make more sense as the context becomes clear.

The History of Prophetic Dreams

Prophetic dreams are as ancient as human civilization itself, stretching back thousands of years across cultures and continents. In many ancient societies, dreams were believed to be messages from the divine or supernatural realm, offering insights into the future, guidance in decision-making, or warnings of impending danger. Accordingly, looking at ancient societies can provide a glimpse into how prophetic dreams are embedded in our wider culture.

Mesopotamia, one of the first civilizations known to exist on the planet, highly valued dream interpretation, enshrining it in their religious and cultural practices. Dreams were direct messages from God, manifestations of divine will, or reflections of the cosmic order illustrating the interconnectedness of the natural and supernatural realms. Dream interpreters, known as "bārû" or "mashmashu," occupied exalted places in Mesopotamian society, serving as advisors to kings, priests, and the public. Tablets exist from Mesopotamia that reflect dream interpretation, including the

"Šumma ālu," with some of these texts dating back to the Old Babylonian period (circa 18th to 16th centuries BCE).

Prophetic dreams' place in religion extends far past Mesopotamia. In Genesis 41, of the Judeo-Christian faiths, Pharaoh has a dream. The dream, vivid and enigmatic, unfolds before Pharaoh's troubled mind; seven plump, majestic cows grazing by the Nile, devoured by seven emaciated, grotesque beasts. Seven ears of robust grain, flourishing under the Egyptian sun, consumed by seven withered husks, parched and lifeless. The imagery is stark, a prophetic tableau painted upon the canvas of Pharaoh's consciousness, foretelling the destiny of Egypt and the fate of its people.

He calls upon Joseph to interpret the dream. Joseph operates as an oracle of divine wisdom, his words imbued with the authority of heaven. He carefully unravels the threads of Pharaoh's dreams, revealing the looming specter of famine that will plague the land for seven years. Yet, in the darkness of impending doom, there shines a beacon of hope—a strategy to navigate the treacherous waters of scarcity and abundance. Joseph's interpretation offers Egypt a lifeline. The granaries swell with abundance during years of plenty, safeguarding against the hardship of future lean years. His insights not only reflect his divine favor but also serve as a beacon of hope for the entire nation. Prophetic dreams also arose in more secular contexts, with Kings replaced with Politicians. The night before Julius Caesar's assassination in 44 BCE, his wife Calpurnia dreamed of his murder and pleaded with him not to attend the Senate meeting. Despite her warning, Caesar went to the Senate where he was assassinated by a group of Roman senators led by Brutus and Cassius. Parallelly, Abraham Lincoln reportedly dreamed that he saw his own body lying in state at the White House. A few days later, on April 14, 1865, he was shot by John Wilkes Booth while enjoying a play in Washington, DC. He died the next day.

The Information in a Dream

A dream lives at the intersection of influence and inference. To properly interpret our dreams, we must be able to break them into these pieces, understanding what is a reflection of our unconscious mind versus what is a manifestation of the collective unconscious. Remember, the collective unconscious is the group of symbols we share as a community united in culture, as proposed by Carl Jung. The biases, influences, and experiences within our unconscious mix with concepts in the collective unconscious in our dreams. The better we understand ourselves, the better we can interpret both the universal (collective unconscious) and personal (our subconscious) meaning within our dreams.

Despite my proficiency in interpreting dreams for others, I can sometimes struggle when interpreting dreams for myself. Many psychologists and psychoanalysts have attempted to create a bible for dream interpretation. I find that, given the unique mix of outside forces and internal messages, dream symbols tend to be shaped by the person experiencing them more than a rigid classification. In using both practice and theory, I've found significant improvements in my ability to interpret both my dreams and those of others.

Understanding both Freudian and Jungian dream interpretation can be helpful. Freudian interpretation tends to be more static, while Jungian interpretation is more dynamic. Both provide frameworks for the psychological underpinnings of dreams and tools for dream interpretation.

From these, we conclude: psychic sensing is the identical twin of the dream: the DNA is the same, but the development is different.

I.   *Freudian Dream Interpretation*

Our favorite daddy Sigmund Freud was one of the first major psychologists to put forward a uniform theory of dream interpretation for the masses. As we have discussed, dream interpretation existed long before Freud. For as long as people have existed, dreams have always felt like a way of a larger entity speaking directly to us, showing us something beyond our typical thought patterns. Still, Freudian theory is the dominating method of dream interpretation.

In his seminal work, *The Interpretation of Dreams*, published in 1899, he proposes a fundamental concept: our dreams are the product of our unconscious minds, expressing things that we may repress in our normal, waking state. While initially believing dreams were mere wish fulfillment, his conceptualization of dreams gradually expanded to the mind processing trauma and fear. Ultimately, he concluded that dreams were prophetic insofar as they represented a wish fulfilled, thus leading us into the future. In short, our dreams are biased by what we desire, but deep meaning still exists within them.

Freud proposes that dreams are made of "manifest content," or the story that the dream is telling, and "latent content," the underlying symbolic meaning of the dream. Symbols are methods for the brain to express its desires, emotions, and conflicts safely. Freud defined many symbols, including:

- Water: the unconscious mind, representing anything from emotion to sexuality to the depths of the unconscious.
- Sexual imagery: repressed desires and sexual anxieties, symbolized by "phallic" objects like snakes and "female" objects like boxes.
- Flying: desire for sexual release, liberation, and transcendence from daily life.
- Teeth: aggression, anxiety about aging and mortality. Losing teeth was akin to powerlessness.
- Being chased: unresolved conflicts, fears, or avoidance of an issue.
- Death: change or transformation, the end of a phase, and the need to move forward.

Symbols were shaped by the individual, despite these larger archetypes, and express nuances of an individual's personal experiences and cultural background. He believed interpretation could also be facilitated by free association, involving exploring the connections between different elements of a dream to uncover underlying thoughts and emotions.

We've explored these concepts before. We see an object and associate it with something deeper through memory recall, just like dream symbolism. We remotely view by focusing on that which lies underneath our objective conscious mind, clearing the way for information to come to us, like reaching the state that allows us to dream. Focusing on the connections between concepts is us following our thought streams, wherever they may go. The "manifest content" of the dream is our little sail catching gusts of intuition, giving us a rough outline of where we must dig deeper.

II.   Jungian Dream Interpretation

I wish to briefly touch on Jungian dream interpretation as well. I find this important as Jung's theories were more nuanced than Freud's...and included a broader frame of reference than "everything means sex." For Carl Jung, a protégé of Freud, a dream is a complex tapestry woven from the threads of personal experiences, unconscious desires, and archetypal motifs permeating throughout the collective unconscious.

A dream bridges the realms of psychology and spirituality with the collective unconscious; the dream's meaning is expressed through symbols both informed by the archetypes in the collective unconscious and in personal experience. For example, the archetype of the Wise Man takes the meaning afforded by the collective unconscious and by the experience of the individual to guide its interpretation.

In introducing the relationship of the collective unconscious to dreams, Jung is linking that which transcends beyond the individual–the collective unconscious being the deep reservoir of human experience shared by all individuals, consisting of universal symbols, themes, and instincts, transcending cultural boundaries and history–to the dream itself.

In a prophetic dream, a precognition or prophecy will offer a glimpse into the collective psyche or future events through symbolism guided by the collective unconscious. Jung believed that synchronicity–the meaningful coincidences that defy conventional explanations of causality–suggests a deeper connection between the inner and outer worlds. This concept, which we as psychics refer to as telepathy and clairvoyance, may manifest when dream imagery aligns with subsequent events. This lends credence to the idea that dreams can serve as channels for accessing intuitive knowledge beyond the limitations of linear time.

With the forces of the collective unconscious and synchronicity influencing dreams, a prophetic dream will arise more frequently during times of psychological or societal upheaval when the collective psyche is stirred by powerful forces or impending changes. For this reason, dreams should not be interpreted literally as they are fundamentally marked by symbolic, psychological, and archetypal aspects. As Cardi B said, "Be careful with me."

III.   Prophecy or Telepathy

As discussed in the chapter on Telepathy, a dream can act as a cable connecting one person to another. This is not a prophetic dream but, rather, a telepathic dream. However, acting on the telepathic dream can bring its context into reality.

In my dream, I see my ex walking down the street. He's trying to stop me to have a conversation. I wake up from the dream, and I do nothing about it. But, later that week, I got an email from my ex.

It's possible that the dream was telepathic: my ex was (either consciously or unconsciously) trying to reach out to me through the dream. When I didn't answer, they (consciously) reached out to me through another medium.

It could also be that the dream was prophetic. My ex was not simply "walking down my street"; he was moving through the places that are home to me in my head, symbolically coming into my energy and reentering my world. With my ex later sending me an email, this dream would prove prophetic–he was trying to reenter my energy.

I did respond to that email from my ex. And later that week, I did symbolically see him in person walking down my street when we started communicating via email. At that moment, the dream also became a premonition in that it told of events replicated from the mental realm into the physical realm.

Psychic sensing and dreams operate so closely along the same pathways, so being *open* to multiple interpretations is crucial–it may be prophetic, it may be telepathic, but you must interpret it as either, neither, and both.

The Dream Versus the Desire

You may be wondering: how can I distinguish between a prophetic dream and my individual desire? Freud said the dream was part of unconscious wish fulfillment! What if I'm just seeing what I want to see?

Good question!

First thing: a prophetic dream *can* be about your own life and desires. But here's a great and easy way to determine whether a prophetic dream is a harbinger of your future or a greater societal event. If the dream does not include you–if you experience it through the eyes of someone else–it is likely that this dream is not about *you*, the individual, and is more about you, as part of a member of society.

When you can be removed from the dream without fundamentally changing its meaning or act mostly as a passive observer within the dream, you are not part of the equation of the dream's message insofar as the dream relates to your future. While your own experiences will still color the interpretation and symbolism in the dream, your role is more of a conduit than a conductor.

In my January 6/George Floyd dream, I experienced it through the eyes of another. I was aware in the dream that I was not occupying my usual body. This signifies that the dream is not about me, the individual, but about society at large, where I am a member, interchangeable with any other member. My impact on the dream was negligible–I was more of an observer. The dream, though, was ultimately interpreted by me and its symbolism unraveled through the lens of my experience.

When you *are* the main character in your dream, it may be a precognitive dream about your own life, or it may be a past-life dream.

If you are the main character in your dream but feel distinctly as if it is not your body, you may be experiencing a past life dream. A past life dream is a reverse prophetic dream–you are looking, but the gaze is to the back. You feel different in the dream because you *are* different. It feels uncanny because you are also intrinsically linked to the main character of the dream. You wear a different guise, different clothing, and are in a different era. But this dream will feel less cryptic–less symbolism-based and more like experiencing a memory which bears little relation to your actual life. It will *feel* personal, even though the contents of the dream are foreign, but no additional context is needed to interpret the dream.

If you are the main character in your dream, and the dream is prophetic, you will need to add the context of the present to arrive at an accurate interpretation. What I've also found is that a dream is more likely to be precognitive when it does not involve the fulfillment of a desire. Let me give an example:

My godmother was sick for a long time, ending up in the hospital for a lung infection. While she was in the hospital, I had a dream (as myself) where she was in a house. I was with her, at her side. She grasped my hand, and I felt her warmth against the relief of her veins. She looked at me and said that she would be fine–that this would pass. Relief passed through my soul; and a weight released. Continuing to clasp my hand, she pulled it tighter. With a firm but light squeeze, she told me what I didn't want to hear: there was a problem with her heart. Her heart, large as it was, would ultimately be her undoing.

Of course, I wanted her to get out of the hospital. I wanted her to recover. I wanted to be around her longer. My desire was for her to live, not for her to be released from the hospital and die from an unrelated condition. That is, however, exactly what happened. My godmother recovered from the lung infection, finally able to come home. We were all positively elated. She died of congestive heart failure later that year.

The dream was prophetic but personal. I was in the dream, so the prediction would define my personal experience, and not impact society at large. The dream did not present the outcome I desired, so my ability to perceive the information was not clouded. The symbolism in the dream and the interpretation were pulled from my own experience. Ultimately, a correct but bleak prediction.

While it is nearly impossible to correctly predict a dream where a desire is fulfilled, if you find yourself in a positive precognitive dream achieving something desired, and the outcome actually happens, then the outcome was predestined. It was meant to be. No interpretation or action could have changed the result. So, maybe it is worth it to put those numbers in your head on a lottery ticket.

I Want One Too!!

Can a prophetic dream be summoned by will? If I really want to know what will happen in the world–whether I want to make a couple stock bets, like those US Senators that made bank by selling stocks after a classified briefing on the threat of Coronavirus–or not, can I make it happen?

Well, yes. But it's not easy.

In Ancient Greek mythology, Apollo established the Oracle of Delphi as a place where Apollo would communicate divine wisdom to mortals. In Delphi, Greece, at the site of Apollo's temple, the Oracle sat. The Oracle was typically chosen from among Apollo's priestesses at the temple. Called the Pythia, she would enter a trance-like, psychoactive state, frequently induced by inhaling vapors rising from a volcanic chasm in the Earth or by chewing laurel leaves, to alter her consciousness. Prophecies would tumble from her mouth in cryptic form before being interpreted by priests, and translated for those seeking the Oracle's guidance. People would come from all around the world seeking a prophecy from the Oracle. Eventually, the Oracle would serve as a consultant on matters ranging from the state to war to personal pursuits.

With the Oracle of Delphi, prophecies could be summoned at will when the Pythia was induced into a certain state and asked directly to give her assessment. Similarly, summoning a prophetic dream is a feat of will and intent. Maybe facilitated by drugs, too, but that'll be in the next book.

Summoning a prophetic dream requires a level of focused intent, much like training for a marathon. It involves meditating for days to hyper-fixate on manifesting the dream–unless you're a lucky person who is naturally in a very focused state of intent. (Luckily for me, I'm now one of those people!)

Before I had my dream about George Floyd, Black Lives Matter, and the January 6 Insurrection of the Capitol Building by neo-fascists, I kept my mind open and focused on what I wanted to know about the future. I needed direction to understand what was happening in my country and to assess threats to my safety. I focused on what I wanted to know, and then it came.

As with so many of the skills mentioned in this book, it takes practice. With practice, your ability to summon a prophetic dream will improve. With practice, your ability to interpret a prophetic dream will improve. With practice, you'll be ready to take your skills confidently anywhere you want to go.

CHAPTER 10

The Psyche to be a Psychic

A Coffee Break

After losing Chelsea and feeling the guilt of failing to give her an accurate reading, Craig, my longtime district manager at Starbucks, left and was replaced by someone whose name I can't even remember. The "family" at work felt hollow, and my satisfaction plummeted. I resolved to commit myself, finally, to starting a full-time business as a psychic. I say "resolved" because I didn't give one of those famous "fuck off, I'm outta here" speeches, burn all bridges, and leave. Before I could be in a place where I'd never look back, I needed to build my getaway car.

With over 10 years of dedicated service as a Starbucks employee, now in management, I earned the ability to take a "Coffee Break." A "Coffee Break" is the opportunity to leave a management position for a year, try something else, and then return if it doesn't work out. Taking a "Coffee Break" gave me a deadline, and having the option to return to my job with enough money saved to cover the year, I avoided making moves out of desperation. If I was going to strike out on my own, I was going to do it in a smart and sustainable way.

Starbucks gave me a Coffee Break, but it also gave me other valuable skills. As a manager, I gained important experience with balancing numbers, making sales, and managing different personalities. Managing also taught me how to approach issues strategically, using structure to maximize outcomes and mitigate problems. After I got rolling, I knew I would be able to handle the financial and personal dimensions.

First, I used my own experiences to build my practice. When I'd gone to other psychics for readings, I found myself dissatisfied with how they spent my time. A psychic would drone on about a "sadness" in my life–45 minutes would pass, and I'd leave with no more knowledge about how to deal with that "sadness" or with any other areas of my life. Never did I want a client to leave a session with me and feel like they'd wasted their time.

Most psychic development books focused on techniques for sensing, not on how to develop a structured technique to produce consistent results. Armed with Starbucks management experience, I designed a structured process with client appointments. Instead of blabbing about whatever information arose through psychic sensing, I kept my inquiries sharp by focusing on four categories: health, finances, career/work, and relationships. The client's goals would inform how we spent their time.

Second, I examined each reading I conducted to find areas of deficiency. Initially, my process involved laying out my oracle cards in a simple formation that would remind me of each category. Then, I'd attempt to sense anything from the cards spread before me. While the readings were more focused than those I'd gotten from other psychics, I still wasn't reaching the depths of details I desired.

Third, I found a mentor. While careful analysis and a unique technique produced results, I wanted to transcend the average street shop psychic, advertising a poster of a palm and crystal ball in their window with the words "psychic reading" scribbled haphazardly above a phone number that looked like it had been changed and rewritten several times. I wanted to build a reputation of "WOW." I wanted to help people handle their past, present, and future.

Since my process wasn't getting me where I wanted to be, Pam Coronado could. Pam Coronado originally entered my life through her television show, "Sensing Murder." She'd walk through different locations of a murder investigation, absorbing details through the energy in each space. Incredibly, she'd use the information gained to formulate a thesis about how the crime happened. A true psychic detective. Most importantly, the specificity of the details she sensed distinguished her from other psychics and mediums. Truly, she modeled an elevated practice and exemplified what good psychic practice could achieve. *That* was what I wanted to be.

OOF. My nerves. I signed up for her first monthly class brimming with anxious anticipation. Pam was a celebrity in the psychic community. Achieving my standard of success necessitated becoming like Pam. I would absorb all that I could from her. In our first weekly group call with her, I was fully star-struck. After several calls, I deciphered Pam's methodology for sensing (she favored a form of remote viewing she learned from her mentors). And, over time, I built a relationship with her. Now, when I'm working with law enforcement to help decipher a crime scene, I can call on her to be a sounding board for my ideas. Not only that, she's become one of my truest and dearest friends.

My greatest hope now is that this book can be for you what Pam was for me. And eventually, I hope that I can be a resource for you, teaching you through my seminars or private sessions and becoming your sounding board, too.

P-PTSD: The Peril of the Psychic

There's PTSD: Post-traumatic stress disorder, associated most closely with singular traumatic events like those experienced during war or a sexual assault. Think "flashbacks" to a specific point in time. There's C-PTSD: complex post-traumatic stress disorder, most closely associated with prolonged traumatic events like childhood abuse or living in a war zone. Think "heightened responses" to certain stimuli not associated with a specific memory. Then, there's P-PTSD: psychic post-traumatic stress disorder. Think of it as a combination of PTSD and C-PTSD. It's the burden carried by a psychic caused by experiencing fully and deeply on behalf of a client.

For career psychics, P-PTSD is also accompanied by a form of ADHD from the brain constantly switching between modes to quickly grab thoughts and process data. Through absorbing client trauma, the brain also becomes more sensitive to a wider array of triggers. But, constantly grabbing information deprives the mind of the ability to properly encode it beyond short-term memory. The psychic mind is the student holed up in the library after a semester of skipping class, desperately flipping through their textbook, panicked, in the hopes of cramming every sentence into their head before their final exam. Simply, the psychic mind can lack the space and grace to recover information.

Being a psychic is draining. You're a phone that keeps ringing, and you're dealing with all types of different callers. In balancing so many distinct personalities, you absorb countless realities and their accordant trauma. You process trauma vicariously and cope with emotions that aren't organically yours. You're a witness to generations of lifetimes of pain. How you respond to this duty will determine your career longevity–and your mental health.

Sensitivity can be a double-edged sword. Burnout is high within the psychic profession, as is self-soothing. Preliminarily, at least from my anecdotal experience, psychics often come from backgrounds marked by significant childhood trauma. Experiencing traumatic conditions from an early age cultivates a heightened sensitivity as a survival mechanism, priming the mind to perceive a wider spectrum of energies. This is clearly advantageous for a profession where success is dependent on picking up the most minute details from a multitude of sources. Additionally, surviving this trauma can foster great resilience, enabling a psychic to endure years of continuous vicarious trauma. On the other hand, they also risk experiencing significant re-traumatization that can be debilitating.

Many psychics find themselves seeking external comfort instead of directly confronting the spoils of profound psychic sensing. Alcoholism. Drug use. Excessive eating. Emotional neglect. Self-harm. Unsurprisingly, long-term indulgence in this type of comfort-seeking will have a side effect of decreasing psychic ability. Sensitivity must be maintained, so finding balance is essential.

The psychic must bend but not break.

FERNANDO MARRON

The Balancing Act

It's clear why failing to adequately address vicarious psychic trauma can cause premature termination of a psychic's ability to practice effectively.

I have unfortunately seen many psychics fall from grace. Some succumb to addiction. Some burn out and become sloppy with their predictions in a misguided attempt at self-preservation; they limit trauma exposure during readings by connecting less, leading to shallow readings marked by decreased accuracy and detail, and extracting income from clients as long as possible. Others, however, completely lose themselves in the systems they believe power their psychic abilities. An individual may focus too intently on the source providing unique credibility to their predictions, neglecting to develop the mental mechanisms and sensitivity necessary for accurate predictions. A person who believes their psychic power derives from angels talking to them may devolve into believing that *all* of their thoughts are messages from angels.

Instead of bursting their reality bubble, they inadvertently create an entirely new one bounded by their delusion.

During the beginning of the COVID-19 pandemic, I saw this numerous times. Just because you've done readings that touch on aspects of health or even *given health predictions* does not mean you're equipped to give health advice, especially on a large scale. Psychics are not gods. Yet, this message did not seem to reach one of my friends. She professed that the cure for COVID came to her in a meditation. Fuck a mask! That's the government trying to use *fear* to control you! All you need to fight this "pandemic" is positive thinking. Try giving yourself ample self-care, listening to your body and giving it what it needs. She didn't need a vaccine, of course, because she had positive thinking. While, in her past practice, she'd made accurate predictions about clients' health outcomes, she couldn't see past herself in her pandemic proclamations. A week after she went public with her argument, she found her husband collapsed on the floor. COVID came for him, and positive thinking couldn't stop his hospitalization.

Another friend that I sincerely admired had a particularly bad COVID take. He was a healer by trade, less known as a traditional psychic and more of a balancer of energy. Maybe he desired to be more than a healer or a desire to boost his perception of self at a time when isolation made most of our lives feel smaller and more ephemeral, but he started using his platform to speak "facts." Those facts were that masks were pointless. He had no background in science and had never worked as a biochemical engineer, pharmacist, epidemiologist, doctor, or even pharmaceutical sales representative. Yet, he knew the answer to the pandemic. He channeled his guides, and they spoke to him. Colloidal silver. So he drank it up, as his "guides"–not the pseudoscientific shillers and vaccine skeptics on social media–told him. Colloidal silver was what the body needed to produce a natural response to COVID. Yet, he ended up with both COVID and heart problems.

Again, none of us are special. We are all humans with the innate capacity to access psychic sensing, a capacity that increases with practice. A psychic may have a different mechanism to do a reading or a different knowledge base to inform readings, but no psychic is a prophet with access to information solely reserved for them. Psychic ability is democratic, not despotic.

Everyone will possess a particular path to prevail against the pathology of their psychic psychosis. Famed psychic John Edwards uses meditation and prayer after each of his sessions. This method did not work on one of my friends. Using prayer and meditation closed him off to the duality of reality, foreclosing him from darker places because his readings are limited by that which he can purge immediately after through prayer and meditation. His readings involve a light touch–a mixture of intuition and good advice–which lead to readings that abut the surface. So much of his focus is on avoiding trauma that he neglects developing his skills further out of fear of what doors it will open. While he journals every morning, his business continues to fail. The difference between him and John Edwards is that John Edwards developed that process as a result of all of his practice, finding out through trial and error what worked for him. Adopting the practice without the process doesn't work.

For me, I practice preventing psychic psychosis by staying grounded and humble. Living in New Mexico affords me year-round access to the beautiful outdoors. Hiking through these divinely scenic passages helps anchor me to the earth, resetting a busy mind. Sex can also be useful–but I would caution against using sex as a way to numb or engage in excess–mindful yet pleasurable engagement is key. To counteract the darkness, keep life curious and playful; yield opportunities to connect with others both inside and outside of the psychic community. Laugh fully, deeply, and shamelessly. Go to comedy shows!

Drugs can be used to turn off or turn on psychic sensing. Drugs may also enable different ways of engaging with yourself by altering the way your brain usually functions, and examining your experiences from a different angle. Only you will know if recreational drugs will be helpful to your practice. Certain recreational drugs, I've found, can enhance sensing abilities by augmenting consciousness expansion. I've found that a good sativa blend can keep the mind active and open during a session. Outside of a reading, drugs can be used to help you step outside yourself, contextualize, and separate mentally from all of the psychological trauma accrued through a day of sessions. Moderation for this type of drug use is key, as engaging in it too frequently can lead to dependence. If legal, recreational drugs like cannabis or psilocybin (in some states) are useful for you and you're able to use them in moderation, please do! Remember, though, at some point, being high is just being high.

Don't Stop Believing

Haters gonna hate.

Say, so the fuck what! The worst thing you can do is to let someone else's opinion of you or what you do overpower what you know to be true about yourself. Don't let your ego get wrapped up in the approval of others. Don't let your trauma be triggered by their rejection. Don't let their limited perspective cause you to abandon your own. You will get better, what you do does have value, and you are worthy of doing what you do. Keep your worth.

PSYCHIC

To be a psychic is to know a skeptic.

People reject what they don't know. There is healthy skepticism. When someone says, "No way!" or makes an ignorant comment like "What's my name?", you will know that you're being confronted with a person curious about the process but unable to articulate that they're looking to understand. Dismiss the skeptical part of them and remember that you're being given an opportunity to educate. They wonder if you can know their name. They wonder what the limits of your abilities are. "Yes, way!"…this is real, this is how it works, and you can do it, too! The only difference between that person and you is years of training, and, well, maybe with some training, you could do what I do even better than I can. And neither of us can read minds.

Sometimes, you're just dealing with an asshole. But, if they're communicating with you or angling for your attention, they're seeking a response. Or maybe, they're just hoping for a reaction. Maybe they think they'll be able to "expose" you. When an asshole like that tries to confront you at a live event, whether it's heckling in person or polluting the comments of a livestream, acknowledge that you're dealing with a shitty person coming from a shitty perspective and constricted to their shitty worldview. Open that asshole up, whether they like it or not. They should know they're part of the psychic community, too, no matter what they profess to be. You don't need to be kind to them. All you need to do is inform them that psychic abilities do not need to conform to society's expectations.

And if this asshole gets you down, remember that curiosity is a marker of intelligence. If this person had any degree of awareness, they wouldn't be such an absolute dumbass.

Albert Einstein–yes, *that*, Albert Einstein–professed a theory of relativity, proclaiming that the fabric of spacetime encompasses all physical events and interactions in the universe. Embedded in this is the phenomenon of "quantum entanglement," wherein entangled particles share correlations regardless of the distance between them. This challenge to conventional "classical physics" causality posits that particles can influence others faster than the speed of light across vast distances. If consciousness exists outside of the physical, it would be able to access information across the space-time continuum; the space-time continuum encompasses all physical events and interactions in the universe. Thus, under quantum entanglement, a non-physical consciousness could hypothetically access all information in the space-time continuum in a manner unconstrained by classical physics.

If you don't understand what that means, it's absolutely okay. All that matters is that the brightest minds entertained theories that support a hypothesis for psychic sensing. So, who the fuck does that asshole stinking up the chat think he is?

Prediction: The Psychic Power

Psychic ability can be utilized in many various avenues. If I were a doctor, I would use it to diagnose. If I were a detective, I would use it to find a lead in the case. The possibilities of doing good with psychic ability are endless. After years of practice, I've been more than able to protect and serve others. Above all, I'm proud of that fact. I believe I provide a net good to the world, even if I get some of my predictions wrong. Even wrong predictions provide an opportunity to learn, grow, and improve.

In practice, I use my readings to serve three primary purposes:

- To give the client a glimpse of something they may experience in the future so they have a chance to prepare for it.

- To give the client a sense of closure, if I'm in a mediumship session.

- To give the client the freedom to expand throughout their own conscious connections, fostering personal growth.

I always make sure that clients understand what I am. I'm not a medical professional. I'm not a legal expert. I'm not a law enforcement official. I'm not a therapist or counselor. I'm not qualified to perform those services. What I am qualified to do is to use my sensing abilities to deduce the foreseeable future.

I've evolved in my practice since the days of four categories and cards. The cards were useful in my early practice because they provided structure, but I felt limited by the amount of data given. Now, when I do a reading, which I call a "Life Reading," I focus on four primary areas to provide structure:

1) HEALTH SCAN

When I meet with a client, I take a long look at them. I ask myself a question: "What is going on here?" Then, I focus in as my brain searches for an answer. Through practice and familiarization with human anatomy, I formulate a 3D model of the person's interior, mentally overlaying it onto them. My intuition will pull me to specific areas. If I see certain objects or symbols in those areas, then I will have an idea of what is going on. If I see electrical wires, I know that's a blood vessel or nervous system issue. If I see an image of Jerry Ryan, I know that there's an issue with the spine. My mind has created this language for me–a shorthand developed from my own experiences that allows me to do an assessment quickly.

With each health scan, I try to give people around 4 to 5 specific issues in their body to keep an eye on. Especially in the USA, we're aware of our health issues, so a client will have more confidence in the rest of the reading because they will already have some indication of my abilities. This allows them to be more open and relaxed for the rest of the reading.

2) FINANCES

The next area I address is personal finances. In our increasingly globalized society, money touches the lives of almost everyone on the planet. I rely on the same syllogistic shorthand for these readings, too. Instead of focusing on the surface, I like to dive deeper. I look at the year ahead like a line graph sensing peaks and valleys. If I see that a person is going to have a financial windfall, I try to determine where that windfall is coming from, if it will be temporary or permanent, or if there's an emotion that will accompany it. At the end of the finances section, I try to give 4 to 5 pieces of practical information about what I'm sensing. I center things like bills, loans, housing, and transportation, so the information will be relevant to their lives. If I sense an amount associated with an event, I will always try to give a ballpark figure.

3) CAREER/JOB

Closely tied to finances, a career/job reading differs because it focuses on the work environment specifically. With my past in both management and front-facing roles, I'm able to understand a range of experiences and have the mental symbolism shorthand for those experiences too. I focus on whether there is a "job" or a "career" for the person. Then, I focus on what their trajectory will be. I stay away from telling people what they *should* do. That's not my role.

4) RELATIONSHIPS

Most people seek a psychic because they want to know about finances or relationships. I've found that relationships are the least interesting part of a reading for me. You could ask me anything, and you want to know…if he's thinking about you? But, it's what they want. I try to provide them with 4 to 5 specific situations to pay attention to in the future, and let them know what's happening, so they can prepare for what they're dealing with. While clients are more likely to accept the reading about the first three categories, they seem least willing to accept relationship readings. They'll try to manipulate me into giving them the answers they want to hear. When this goes too far, I'll say, "If your intuition is so great, why are you even going to a psychic?" My job is not to fight with them. It is to tell them what I sense, even if it isn't the prettiest picture.

Finally, I end my readings by asking my clients if they have any additional questions. I try to make sure my clients always feel heard. If they seek something that I can't confidently answer, I'll let them know and tell them what I *can* say. For example, a client may beg me to tell them if they're going to win the lottery or not. If I can't sense that, I'll focus on whether I see their finances increasing or not. Every prediction is an interpretation of the symbols and senses

I receive during a reading. Some of the scenarios I share may be out of context or the specifics different from reality, but I can still pinpoint the details and associated circumstances.

I share all of this for the same reasons I wrote this book. I want to emphasize the responsibility that comes with psychic practice, I want you to recognize that the seed of psychic ability has always been within you, and I want you to trust in your capacity to unlock its full potential to create change in the world. You are psychic.

You always were, and you always will be.

GET OUT THERE AND USE IT!

I'll be in these pages and in real life if you ever need any help.

A Few Past Predictions

Now, I'm going to be open with you like I am with the world when I post my predictions publicly on social media, @fernyesp on TikTok and Instagram/Threads, and on my website, fernandomarron.com. Some predictions are wholly accurate, some are mostly accurate, some have a few missed or incorrect details, and some are completely wrong. But I hope that this is evidence to support the idea that psychics can be extremely accurate when their abilities are taken seriously, honed over time, and used for the public good.

Here's a sampling of a few of my past predictions, the good, the bad, and the ugly:

DATE	PREDICTION	OUTCOME
July 31, 2014	Prediction regarding Ebola vaccine, posted on Facebook: "PREDICTION: At the end of 2015, early 2016 a possible treatment/vaccine for the prominent strain of Ebola virus will be developed. It affects/focuses on the protein makeup of the virus. The idea for the treatment/vaccine comes from an already being tested/utilized concept around another major illness/disease." 	ACCURATE 12/23/2016: Ebola vaccine created by scientists at the National Microbiolog y Laboratory in Winnipeg, Canada. Hundreds of thousands have since been vaccinated
July 31, 2014	Prediction regarding same-sex marriage, posted on Facebook:	ACCURATE 06/26/2015: *Obergefell* is

	"PREDICTION: in the late spring, early summer May/June of 2015, a high court ruling will legalize same sex marriage in states like Texas, possibly affecting all 50 states."	decided, legalizing same-sex marriage in all states

August 12, 2014	Prediction regarding Mexican Cartel routes usage by terrorists, posted on Facebook: "PREDICTION: in the coming two years we will become publicly aware of terrorist extremist groups collaborating with the Mexican Drug lord organizations in an effort to buy their way into the United States through existing drug smuggling	ACCURATE. July 11, 2020: U.S. South Command warns that Sunni Extremists are infiltrating

	operations and channels across the U.S./Mexico Border."	the Southern Border	

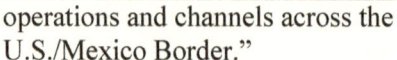
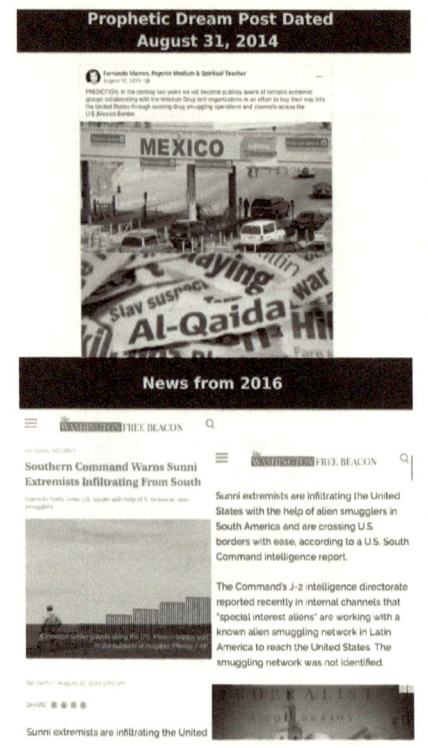

When I made this prediction, I thought it would happen within two years. The elements of my prediction were all there, but the timing was off.

| July 8, 2017 | Prediction regarding domestic terrorist activity in a public performance space in a dry climate, posted on YouTube:

"there's some theatre or maybe movie complex that is going to be targeted by possibly terrorist, maybe local terrorist. Umm and they're going to either sabotage or they're going to place some objects in the theatre that may blow up and are going to affect several individuals in that theatre. People will still be able to get out alive but they're gonna be | ACCURATE.

10/03/2017:

Domestic terrorist gunman opens fire at an outdoor country music concert in Las Vegas, Nevada; over |

a lot of people that are hurt or that are affected by the theater and it is a drier climate so I'm assuming it's in some sort of dryer area or an arid area like Arizona or Nevada. Um…um… just a dryer cause I kept seeing that all that dry aired region and then the color scheme was like… like orangey, reds and whites um… in the theatre and it was like an old style theater so it could be a movie theater, could be a performance theatre."

500 hurt and 58 dead; materials to make explosives found in gunman's vehicle and home.

Video Prediction Dated July 8, 2017

Terrorist Dreams

" there's some theatre or some movie complex that is gonna be targeted by possibly terrorist, maybe local terrorists. Umm and they're going to either sabotage or they're going to place some objects in the theatre that may blow up and are going to affect several individuals in that theatre. People will still be able to get out alive but they're gonna be a lot of people that are hurt or that are affected by the theater and it is a drier climate so I'm assuming it's in some sort of dryer area or an arid area like Arizona or Nevada. Umm.. um.. just a dryer cause I kept seeing that all that dry and region and then the color scheme was like… like orangey, reds and um whites umm.. in the theatre and it was like an old style theatre so it could be a movie theatre, could be a performance theatre. " Ferny Statement

Events of October 3rd, 2017

January 29, 2020	Prediction regarding the Kobe Bryant Helicopter crash, posted on YouTube: "Again, it may come out as if it is a pilot error or it's the pilot's fault." "So I don't think this would have been a pilot issue. It was definitely an equipment issue." "Which there's already going to be two separate lawsuits in regard to this situation." 	PARTIALLY ACCURATE. 09/22/20: Vanessa Bryant files two separate lawsuits regarding the death of Kobe Bryant and her daughter, one against the LA County Sheriff and another against the pilot. 02/09/21: Investigators determine pilot error at fault for Kobe's helicopter crash.
NFL	2021: Prediction of Buccaneers victory in Super Bowl (Facebook)	2021: Buccaneers 31, Chiefs 9

Super Bowls	2022: Prediction of a Chiefs victory in Super Bowl (Facebook) 2024: Prediction that 49ers would be winning until the last second (Instagram Live) 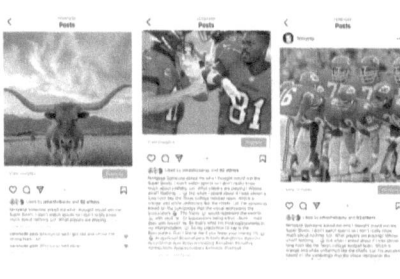 	2022: Rams 23, Bengals 20 2024: Chiefs 25, 49ers 22 in Overtime
January 29, 2021	Prediction regarding a Russian power struggle "Within 2-3 years there may be a significant shift in the geological trends of Russia, with the power struggle between Putin, the government & wealthiest individuals & organizations in the country. This may also include a change of government control or power away	ACCURATE February 2022: War in Ukraine; Russian economy faces meltdown because of sanctions;

	from the current political leanings. The Russian central bank and the decentralization of assets and trading potentials may be at the center of an advancing revolution that may start with existing protesting platforms & agendas. A back and forth between the government vs. the wealthiest in the country may become apparent as financial gains may be lost through effects from currency, digital cryptocurrencies, assets, and trading opportunities, as well as economical moratorium. It may seem like the government makes a misstep costing the population, country, and wealthiest significantly which could further revolutionize existing political trends and the established population/power base. This could be a gradual build up of tensions as the economy attempts to recover itself and significant opportunities lost. #russia #putin #wealth #trade #cryptocurrency #revolution #powerstruggle"	US Banks and Binance bar Russians and central bank from accessing reserves; concerns that oligarchs are turning on Putin because of losing battle in Ukraine